WHEN ROCKS CRY OUT!

Explosive secret uncovered:
An ancient Egyptian city called
Jerusalem, in South America!

HORACE BUTLER

STONE RIVER PUBLISHING
Fort Worth, Texas

Second Edition, published 2009

Printed in the United States of America

1 3 5 7 9 10 8 6 4 2

Library of Congress Cataloging-in-Publication Data
Butler, Horace
When rocks cry out / Horace Butler
Spirituality
Religion, Old Testament
America, Pre-Columbian
Egypt, ancient

ISBNS: 978-0-615-29265-6

In loving memory of

the beautiful Gwendolyn Joyce Butler, *my wife,*
who loved me and guided me with her wisdom;
and,

Damon, *my first born, whose extraordinary spirit*
found its way to Heaven
much too soon.

ACKNOWLEDGMENTS

My special thanks go to Myrtle Josephine Bardere-Smith and James Thomas Smith of New Orleans for their considerable encouragement through the gift they provided, which made this book possible.

What thanks can I offer to the great spirit of Dr. Ivan Van Sertima, who spoke with me more than any other scholar, encouraging me and guiding me to not be blinded by pride and racial ignorance? He opened the door for an entire world to see its secret childhood.

Always I must acknowledge my father Horace Butler and my mother Josephine Smith-Butler. Without their courage and love, this book certainly could not have been written.

To Janice Denise Pyron, Rose Mitchell and "the angel of the ruffled wings," Lynn Smith, please accept my deepest thanks. Without your love and your encouragement, my burden would have been unbearable.

I bow my head in deep respect to Lola Onick, the most constant angel, whom I share with so many. Your poise, your grace, these strengthen me.

My heartfelt appreciation goes to The Road Crew, that group of musicians who 'watered' my soul while I crossed the Atacama Desert of my life.

Finally, to Brandon Robinson, maybe one day we can explain the full meaning of the intriguing cover you created for this book. So many degrees past Da Vinci!

Chapter 1

"Of Angels and Demons"

A bloody butcher knife lay near her covered body. He had stabbed her, clubbed her to death . . . and raped her. He signed his name, in blood, with the "Star of David." He said that he was an angel from god, sent to kill people who did not deserve to live. He said he had murdered people in Texas, Kentucky, Illinois and other places, hopping on trains, riding in boxcars, to reach his victims, usually killing them in their homes.

Not far from a line of railroad tracks, he stole into the home of a preacher and his wife, and then he brutally bashed in their heads with a sledgehammer, while they slept. Near another set of tracks, he left a pickax stuck between the eyes of an elderly woman.

Now he had said he was headed to Dallas.

The young FBI agent sat across the desk from me, examining the encrypted internet messages that seemed to show that a fanatical religious group had curious knowledge about the serial killer's movements. I had happened upon the internet site while searching to see if professors were discussing discoveries I had shared with them. I had typed in my name and "Jerusalem."

I looked out the glass windows of the Cash America building. *Why would the FBI lease office space from a pawn shop chain?*

"You say you got these from the internet?" the agent asked.

"Yes."

"And you think he may be coming to harm you, because you've found ancient records about Egypt building a city called Jerusalem . . . in South America?

The way he said the words made the idea seem absurd. The fanatics certainly knew of me and had sent a woman to investigate me at the used-books store where I spent hours searching for pieces of the *"forbidden histories,"* as the secret writings were called. Then there were the internet messages they had sent to my computer.

The agent hardly looked at me. We briefly discussed comments about two of the murders. He tried hard not to show any interest in the manuscript that lay on the desk near my hand, but his eyes stole quick, short glances at the bound pages that held the discoveries. Suddenly, he stood and ushered me to the elevator. "We do thank you for bringing this to our attention."

"You *are* going to do something with this?" I asked. "You see where he is. He's right there!"

"All I can tell you is to be sure to look over your shoulders."

Look over my shoulders? I studied his face, attempting to decipher what he was thinking about the notes I had brought. Maybe he thought I was being paranoid. The elevator doors closed, fencing me in with a strange feeling that was ballooning in my chest.

10

I walked out of the tall glass building into the blinding Texas summer sun that seared the asphalt of the parking lot. Strangely, I hoped I *was* being paranoid. Still, I reached beneath the driver's seat and disengaged the safety on the long, chrome barreled .45 that a friend had given me when he heard the killer was heading toward Dallas.

I took a deep breath, trying to loosen the tightness in my chest. Then I shoved the heavy gun beneath a newspaper on the passenger seat. *The President of my country had been murdered just 30 miles from where I lived. They had chosen Dallas for a reason.*

I tried to shake the thought from my head. It didn't work. I exhaled, hard. Moving the shifter into gear, I headed home. *At least there is a record now. My government can't say they didn't know about them.*

Chapter 2

"Fear in the temple"

Pushing apart the Venetian blinds with my fingers, I scanned the cars parked in front of the double windows. The old El Dorado coupe was gone. They were family. They never told me they were there. I would just see the two heads leaned deep into the seats, their eyes staring straight toward my window. When night rolled in, they did too. Now it was dawn and they were gone.

Walking quickly to the car with the package in my hand, my eyes searched the iron grates of the fence 20 yards to my right. Beyond the fence stretched a quarter-mile of open field, with a railroad running through it.

I had decided that I needed to get the secrets into the hands of others. There was one man who seemed ready to receive them.

Ten minutes later, I pulled onto the lot across the street from the church. I parked and waited.

Several women, some walking unsteadily on their high heels, cautiously picked their way around small puddles of rainwater. I thought I had timed my arrival late enough to find the preacher adjourned to his office. I had arrived too early.

I couldn't wait any longer.

Entering the foyer, I waded through the crowd to get to the preacher before he left the church. Hundreds of people pressed their way out of the sanctuary, where the large bulk of a man stood wide-legged and smiling as he received a line of people who wanted to speak with him or to congratulate him on his sermon.

After several minutes, the line before the preacher ended. I saw him squinting his eyes to better pierce the darkness at the back of the sanctuary, where I stood. Finally, I would get to ask him what he thought of the manuscript I had left with him three weeks earlier.

When I approached him, his smile widened and he extended his hand. He didn't say anything immediately. Then he looked away from me and said, "I read the book. What you have found is just amazing."

He pointed to someone near the podium and told him to get the manuscript from the preacher's office.

Then he continued, "I actually read the book more than once. The first time I read it, I was reading to dispute what was in it. You know, I was reading with the understanding of things I have learned during my years in the ministry. But every time I came up with a question that would prove the book was wrong, something in the book would answer it. I mean, I would be reading, and I would see something, and say, 'Aha! This can't be right,' because of something I knew. Then, later in the book, I would see the answer. Every time I came up with a question, I would read a little further and there was the answer. After that, I read the book again to understand what was there. I think every preacher should see this. The book is extraordinary!"

That was promising, but there was still the question of whether he would help to get the findings announced. I did not have to wait long for the answer. The person returned with the manuscript and gave it to me. The preacher spoke again.

"Do you know you have World War III there in your hands?"

I studied his expression for any sign that he was jesting, that he was not serious about what he had said. Before I could decipher his meaning, he laughed.

He had read the findings. *Didn't he realize how important the discovered things were to Christianity?* I probed again, trying to determine if he really knew what the findings meant.

"Don't you think people, especially Christians, should know these things? It all changes now. We have been looking in the wrong places!"

"Well, you are going to need some people who have more power than I have, to get these things known," answered the preacher. "You need somebody like Jakes to help with this. I know I can get a meeting with them about this."

Before I realized it, my head had motioned against the idea of seeking help from the Dallas preacher. He had been one of the first preachers to receive memos about the discoveries.

"I've already tried to speak with him about the findings," I told him.

"You can't just walk up to Jakes," he admonished. "That man has a room filled with proposals that people send to him. Everybody wants a piece of him now. He doesn't have time to read all those things. But he knows me, and I can introduce him to this work. He'll give it a look then. It may not be soon, but he'll look at it."

I was told to expect a call within two weeks, and then the meeting ended.

I didn't have the promise of support I had come for, but I did have one more promise to hope against.

Chapter 3

"A storm over Egypt"

Torrents of rain slammed against the windshield quicker than the wipers could clear the blurring water.

I looked at the manuscript on the seat next to me.

"Do you know you have World War III there in your hands?"

I shook my head. Several weeks had passed. I would not hear from the preacher again. I knew that, but I didn't want to believe it. I was running out of ways to get the discoveries announced.

I had seen ancient records that unveiled the world's most explosive secret. 'Egypt' had crossed the Atlantic Sea, in ships, more than 10,000 years before the time of Christ. They had built the world's largest cities, in South and Central America, and in Mexico They had united those city-states into a nation that stretched from Brazil in South America to Mexico, and into Africa. I had broken the seal on the *'forbidden histories.'* I had found the writings that told how Egypt had built its most powerful empire, and it had happened in the Americas. Three of the world's most powerful religions had come out of Egypt, and now their most fearful secret was uncovered.

More disturbing to some, I had gotten the old maps that showed where the ancient Egyptian cities had stood, in the Americas.

Ancient writings, including an autobiography left by Moses, explained that a civil war in Central and South America had forced the 'Egyptians' to flee from the Americas. They escaped to the east side of Africa, where they built a second Egypt. That was not, however, the discovery the preacher was thinking of when he called the findings "World War III." He had seen the city that ancient Egypt had built in a mountain in South America. It was this city that had stirred his fears, and his reluctance.

Ancient Egyptians had named that capital city, 'HERU,' to keep alive the name of one of Egypt's founding kings. The city Heru was eventually called Heru-Salem, then Jeru-Salem, and it had stood in the Americas. It was the presence of ancient Egypt's Jerusalem, in the Americas, that kept scholars quiet, and preachers fearful, when I showed them the old maps and the ancient writings . . . and the *forbidden histories*.

There were others who knew the *forbidden histories*. Even Christopher Columbus knew these secrets. He wrote that South America's Orinoco River flowed out of "Paradise," where Adam and Eve had lived. I was stunned to see that Columbus had promised he would recapture Jerusalem when he reached the Americas.

The illuminati knew the secrets. They quietly discussed the $10 million Waldseemuller Map that was made in 1507. They whispered that the mapmaker Martin Waldseemuller revealed things on that map that were not to be revealed. The map was famed for the "impossible" details about the Americas that it showed. It even revealed the Pacific Ocean, before it was "re-discovered" by Europeans, who had lost knowledge of the Americas after being expelled from the Western Hemisphere during the Dark Ages. Waldseemuller admitted he had gotten information to make the map of the Americas from works left by ancient Egypt!

Waldseemuller removed the name, *America*, when he published the map again. Some believed Waldseemuller had been forced to remove the name that Egypt had given to the Americas, along with other curiously accurate details about "the New World."

The illuminati wasted no time debating whether the name *America* was taken from the name of the explorer Amerigo Vespucci. Those enlightened ones knew that the Vespucci lie was a ruse to hide the secret about Egypt and its naming of the Americas. Their strategy of silence had kept the forbidden secrets intact, even when strangers had happened upon pieces of the secrets.

But now, Isaiah's prophecy was beginning to breathe. A storm was gathering. Cries from ancient stones in Egypt were rising through the old valleys of the dead and up to the clouds. Rocks were crying out a secret that thundered and trembled through even "anointed" men, who could not make their mouths say the secrets.

The gatekeepers were scrambling desperately to restore the *'seal'* on secrets they thought they had buried forever. They thought they had destroyed Christianity, with a man called Da Vinci, and a supposed "Code." Now it was Christianity's turn, and Isaiah's turn, to unleash the real "secret" behind the real "Code."

Chapter 4

"Isaiah's prophecy: they will 'seal' the knowledge"

"Hello? Can I help you?"

His voice sounded familiar. I asked the man's name, wanting to know if I had gotten the same person at the Institute who had spoken to me before.

He answered that it was him. Now I could ask him the question again.

"We spoke some months ago about ancient Egypt being in the Americas. Do you remember—"

"I remember the conversation."

"You do?"

"Yes," he replied, sounding annoyed.

"Sir, you said at that time that there was nothing that could convince you ancient Egypt had been in the Americas. Have you heard of the PBS documentary, *The Cocaine Mummies?*"

"Yes. I've heard of it."

"And that didn't change anything in your thinking about ancient Egypt and the Americas?"

"No. No one took those findings seriously. They were never published in a medical journal as scientific fact."

I fingered through the pages of notes in front of me.

"Mr. Jones, I can give you citations to two medical journal articles about the discovery of South America's cocaine in ancient Egyptian mummies. Those findings have been published by the scientists."

"It doesn't matter. I've got to go."

"The discovery of *COCAINE*, deep within the tissues of ancient Egyptian mummies—including a Pharaoh—doesn't open your thinking about ancient Egypt being in the Americas?"

"No, it doesn't. I'm sorry, but I've got to go now."

That conversation opened my eyes, wide. I would waste no more time with so-called scholars. I had read the biblical narratives called *Isaiah*. This Jerusalem prophet had written that "learned" scholars would attempt to hide the knowledge, by "sealing" the knowledge—by refusing to tell the true meanings of the writings. Isaiah wrote:

"And the vision of all is become unto you as the words of a book that is sealed, which men deliver to one that is learned, saying, Read this, I pray thee: and he saith, I cannot; for it is sealed: And the book is delivered to him that is not learned, saying, Read this, I pray thee: and he saith, I am not learned.

"Wherefore the Lord said...I will proceed to do a marvellous work among this people, even a marvellous work and a wonder: for the wisdom of their wise men shall perish, and the understanding of their prudent men shall be hid.

"Woe unto them that seek deep to hide their counsel from the LORD, and their works are in the dark, and they say, Who seeth us? and who knoweth us? Surely

20

your turning of things upside down shall be esteemed as the potter's clay: for shall the work say of him that made it, He made me not? Or shall the thing framed say of him that framed it, He had no understanding?

"Is it not yet a very little while, and Lebanon shall be turned into a fruitful field, and the fruitful field shall be esteemed as a forest? And in that day shall the deaf hear the words of the book, and the eyes of the blind shall see out of obscurity, and out of darkness."

Had the scholars never read Isaiah? Didn't they know the prophecy Isaiah had left about them?

I tossed the car into a U-turn across the rain slick pavement, splitting the traffic. Straightening the car into a lane, I sped back home.

When I passed through the door of the house, I dropped my knees to the carpet in front of a chair and folded my soul into a prayerful pose. I wrapped my fear and frustrations within a blanket of words, handed them to God in thought, and lingered there, with my head in my hands, for nearly half an hour. When I arose from the carpet, I had a will to do nothing but sit there in the darkness.

For all the grace that had come my way, I felt I had gotten nothing done. My friends ran from the sight of me. I had tried everything I knew, but I was unsuccessful in letting the world hear of its buried heritage. The exhaustion and despair of the last two years were at that very moment attempting to strangle my hope. The room darkened with the arrival of dusk and I sat there, wrapped in that black quiet. For hours I sat there. I could not remember another day in my life when I felt so alone.

Then something compelled me to rise. I got back into the car and soon found myself standing in a bookstore. I should not have been there. I had no interest in reading one more word. I was full of words. Yet, here I stood, surrounded by millions of screaming words.

I had never visited the magazine stand in that store, and I had never read a *Biblical Archaeology Review* magazine, but now that magazine was in my hands.

Chapter 5

"Jerusalem is missing!"

I parted the pages of the magazine until I reached the featured article. Instantly the words streamed through my eyes and began flooding my brain with blood. I could feel my heart beating inside my head. When I focused and understood the words that blackened the page before me, my breath went still.

The words in the magazine announced a discovery by archaeologist Dr. Margreet Steiner in an article called "It's Not There." Here is a portion of that courageous announcement as it appeared in the July-August, 1998 issue of the *Biblical Archaeology Review*.

"The history of Jerusalem is going to have to be rewritten. As we gradually assimilate the archaeological record, we are finding more and more evidence that calls into question long-held assumptions about the city's past. This is especially true of the three periods I will discuss ... The history of these periods is particularly sensitive in that it ultimately involves the historicity of the glorious reigns of David and Solomon—at least, according to the Bible—and the existence of the United Monarchy of Israel.

"...Failure to publish the evidence from the large excavations conducted in Jerusalem since 1960 has created severe problems for scholars who wish to evaluate the Jerusalem of these periods. The directors of all four major excavations died without writing final reports. ...Not one final report from these excavations has been completed, although teams of archaeologists are now working on them in Jerusalem; Manchester, England; and Leiden, the Netherlands.

"...The history of Jerusalem in the Late Bronze and Iron Age is usually based on an analysis of written sources—the Bible and some archaeological texts and documents, such as the 14th-century BCE Amarna letters from Egypt. Archaeological materials from Jerusalem itself are then used to clarify and confirm this picture. However, I shall proceed here from the opposite direction, starting with the archaeological evidence from the site.

"Most of the Late Bronze Age material recovered from Jerusalem has come from tombs, especially one on the Mount of Olives that contained hundreds of pots, mainly of local ware, and from a pit south of the city, which held some pottery and a scarab. North of the Old City, the remains of what may have been an Egyptian temple were also excavated.

"But no remains of a town, let alone a city, have ever been found: not a trace of an encircling wall, no gate, no houses. Not a single piece of architecture. Simply nothing!"[i]

No prayer I could have put together would have been bold enough to ask for what I had just seen.

In the same magazine that announced Steiner's "missing" Jerusalem report, another archaeologist attempted to remove the great significance from Steiner's

24

historic revelation. He argued that ancient letters found in Egypt, and written from an Egyptian king of Jerusalem to the Egyptian Pharaoh, prove Jerusalem existed as an important city even before David built his great, monumental city. To strengthen his argument against the discovery that Jerusalem was missing, he then listed several other famed biblical cities whose ruins did not show a city.

Some scholars reasoned that Egyptian letters, discussing Jerusalem before the time of David, made it indisputable that Jerusalem existed north of Africa during the time of David and Solomon. To those scholars, no matter what the archeological proof showed, Jerusalem absolutely *had* to be on that hill in the Middle East.

Their reasoning seemed sound, but it was wrong. Their reasoning failed to consider that Jerusalem *did* exist during that time, but at a different place.

According to several ancient historians, Jerusalem was one of the largest, richest cities in the ancient world—especially during the time of David and Solomon. One of the greatest cities built in the earth was entirely missing in the dirt and scholars were pointing to pieces of a pot as proof Jerusalem had been on that hill.

Failing to consider that ancient Jerusalem was at a different place than the hill now going by that name, the scholars entrapped themselves into establishing, erroneously, an entire biblical landscape around a hill where ancient Jerusalem was entirely missing.

How discomforting it could be to realize the Old Testament events had occurred in a land that was nearly halfway round the world from the places propped up by the scholars' astounding mistakes.

I included the Steiner article and rushed the discoveries to a major publisher who had requested them during a call that had gotten past his assistant. Less than two weeks later, the manuscript was back in my hands. A cover letter from the vice president of the company explained:

"I'm afraid I just wouldn't have the necessary background to edit your manuscript intelligently. But thanks for the look."

The Steiner confirmation regarding Jerusalem did not set aflame the interest of the publisher. I finally understood that confirmation of the discoveries was not the problem. Something else was keeping this biblical history veiled in secrecy—and in silence.

I wondered, *Was it the same fear that had also kept them from mentioning Sarah Kali, when they had run to fly the rumor about Mary Magdalene? SARAH KALI*—the name means *"black princess." What skin on parents is needed to produce a "black skinned" daughter? A Black Magdalene? A Black Christ? Both?*

They had found the courage to try to destroy the Christ, but their strength withered when they reached the black skinned girl, Sarah Kali.

So they erased Sarah Kali from their supposed "book of codes." But it was too late. They had opened *Pandora's Box*, and now they could not close it again. Jerusalem was coming down from the mountain.

Chapter 6

"The thread that led to the stones"

Always, they ask me the question, "Why are you doing this—what made you start looking for this?"

The secret histories unfolded during my search for an early group of people in North America known as "the Kali." A public television (PBS) documentary, *The History of the American West,* mentioned that early Spanish explorers found a people called Kali living in the western reaches of the North American continent. The documentary made no other mention of the Kali after revealing these early Americans to be "black."

I had never heard of the Kali, or of any other black-skinned people, being in America when Columbus came.

I sent e-mails to PBS asking for the sources that told of the Kali. I got no response. I searched the Internet for the *History of the American West* documentary and found an excerpt from that project, but there was no reference to the Kali.

Weeks passed and, still, not one single sentence was found about the American Kali. I would try one last time. The documentary said the early Spanish explorers saw the Kali, so I decided to concentrate on the period when Spain began its exploration of the Americas.

Almost immediately, my fortune changed. Rare books and maps of the Southwest region of North America were found in the Special Collections Library at a local university. Maybe I would find something about the Kali in those maps and records.

Arriving at this library, I discovered there were numerous old maps and records about the period and place where the Spanish explorers saw the Kali. I was fortunate to meet a Hispanic librarian who possessed deep knowledge of historical Spanish literature, which included some of the most detailed descriptions of the "New World" and its people.

She knew the records that preserved Spain's early descriptions of the Americas. After being introduced to her, I went straight to the riddle that had consumed me. "I'm looking for the black people called Kali who were in the Americas when the conquistadors arrived."

The slight smile fell from the librarian's mouth. She glanced about the dimly lit room, apparently to determine if anyone overheard my question. She walked me quickly to a table, away from the ears of the few people near the entrance.

"I can tell you where to find the Blacks who were in America when Columbus came here," she whispered, as she leaned toward me for confidentiality. "But, you do understand that people do not like to talk about that, don't you?"

She did not wait for an answer.

"I know there were several groups of Blacks here, and not just in the islands, but in South America, too," she offered, while occasionally looking around as though we were committing a grave conspiracy.

"They were called the Caribs, the Black Caribs," she said.

We talked a few minutes longer, then she told me to come back the next day and she would give me a list of books and authors to research.

The next day, I met her during lunch. She gave me the folded computer printout that listed several books, including some books written in Spanish. Then she pointed to some of the books on the list and told me what each could offer. One was written from the viewpoint of "the common person"; while another was composed to be a formal government publication. She also mentioned someone named "Sahagun," and "Castillo." She whispered at length about the explorer Castillo. He could be trusted to give an accurate account of things. She barely mentioned Sahagun, but a serious look stoned across her face when she said his name. She made sure I understood, "Sahagun is *the* authority."

After several more minutes of explanations about the works and writers of the Spanish conquest of the Americas, she wished me luck, and I was left with the paper trail of books.

Taking the elevator down to the main library, I decided to concentrate on the books written by Castillo and the other conquistadors. I had to hurry. My lunch hour was running out of minutes.

My eyes and fingers raced each other across the spines of the books, searching hurriedly for two of the books the librarian had pointed to on the printout. Neither book was in its slot. I grabbed a book that stood where one of the missing books should have been.

"The Letters of Cortes."

I thought the title sounded too innocent to hold any hope of a dramatic expose concerning a lost nation of people, but I wanted to get started and *The Letters* would have to do. My lunch hour had vanished.

Back at the office, I scanned the first few chapters of the book, and I was sure nothing of importance would be found there.

After work, I returned to the library and found several more titles that were on the printout. I checked out several of them. Now, if one book had nothing on the Kali, I would have others that would allow me to continue the search. For whatever reason, when I checked out the other books, I did not give back *The Letters*.

When I arrived home, I, again, found myself opening *The Letters of Cortes,* which described the war against the Aztecs. Hernando Cortes, the leader of the Spanish invasion, wrote these so-called "letters."

Deep into the night, I was fighting off sleep to squeeze in more of the pages from *The Letters* and from another book. I was glued to two separate accounts of the invasion of Mexico. Something was pulling me through the texts and I could not stop. I was only vaguely aware that rooms in the house had quietly turned black as the family fainted into sleep. I never heard the call to dinner.

It was nearly midnight and I was trying to absorb the view of the Valley of Mexico through the writings of the Spaniards. I was not doing a good job that night. I kept falling under the hypnotic persuasions of sleep, but I had to keep at it. I felt as if something was near and it was going to show itself that night.

Then I saw it! My eyes jerked open and tried to focus. My eyes traced over the words again, this time slowly. I shut the book and walked outside into the cool night air. Several deep breaths pulled the sting of the night air across my insides, and the sluggish ropes of sleep began to loosen.

It was a few minutes past midnight. Nearly all the lights in the neighborhood had fallen asleep, but it was time for me to wake up. I walked back inside from the brisk night air and split open the book to the statement that had pulled me from the spell of sleep. The words in the statement had come from the Aztec leader Montezuma. This is what I saw:

"Long time have we been informed by the writings of our ancestors that *neither myself nor any of those who inhabit this land are natives of it, but rather strangers who have come to it from foreign parts.* We likewise know that from those parts our nation was led by a certain lord (to whom all were subject), and who then went back to his native land, where he remained so long delaying his return that at his coming those whom he had left had married the women of the land and had many children by them and had built themselves cities in which they lived, so that they would in no wise return to their own land nor acknowledge him as lord; upon which he left them. And we have always believed that among his descendants one would surely come to subject this land and us as rightful vassals. Now seeing the regions from which you say you come, which is *from where the sun rises,* and the news you tell of this great king and ruler who sent you hither, we believe and hold it certain that he is our natural lord: especially in that you say he has long had knowledge of us."[iiii]

31

I marked the page, turned toward the group of books on the bed, and pulled out the book written by Cortes' secretary, Francisco Gomara. Opening Gomara's account to the same meeting between Cortes and Montezuma, I read to see what he wrote about Montezuma's words to Cortes. Gomara wrote:

"…As my father told me, and his father told him, our ancestors and kings, from whom I am descended, were not natives of this country, but newcomers, led by a great lord who, a little while later, returned to his own land."[iv]

The Aztecs were *foreigners* who came to America aboard ships, which had come from the direction, "…where the sun rises."

Montezuma's speech astonished me.

This was a critically important correction of pre-Columbian American history by Montezuma, whose name was really "Motecuhzoma," according to the Aztecs.

Most modern historians deny, passionately, a trans-Atlantic origin for the Aztecs, claiming the Aztecs were Indians who migrated from North America. How had these historians missed seeing what Motecuhzoma had said?

I slid back into the pages of the letters Cortes had written to the King of Spain. This military leader had taken ships and troops from a harbor at Cuba, without the Spanish king's permission, and had begun waging war against people in Mexico, including the Aztecs. Cortes' "letters" did not seem, really, like letters. Instead, they were a sort of brief, providing detailed accounts of

what Cortes saw, heard, and did during his attack on
Mexico.

Sometime during the reading, sleep folded itself back
across me, and I melted into the morning.

The next night, I was back into the colors and smells
of the Aztec capital. Just after midnight, another curious
passage came from Cortes' 'Letters':

" ... and so we remained there very much at ease
throughout the rest of that day and night thinking that all
disturbance had settled down. Next day after hearing
mass I despatched [sic] a messenger to Vera Cruz giving
them the good news that I had entered the city to find
the Christians [Spanish soldiers] alive and the city now
quiet. But in half an hour he returned all covered with
bruises and wounds, crying that the whole populace of
the city was advancing in war dress and all the bridges
were raised. And immediately behind him came a
multitude of people from all parts so that *the streets and
house-roofs were black with natives;* all of whom came on with
the most frightful yells and shouts it is possible to
imagine." [v]

"*...the streets and house-roofs were black with natives...*"

The attack had occurred after sunrise. The blackness
of the Aztec warriors was not the result of night's lack of
light. Cortes' slip of the tongue regarding the blackness
of the Aztecs was followed a few days later by another
comment that slipped through the censors.

"There are cormorants also, marvelously skillful in
fishing, and a bird that looks like a swan, only its neck is
much longer and more strange; and pelicans of many
colors that live by fishing, as big as geese, with a beak
about two spans long, only the lower member of which

is movable, with a sack that hangs down to their breast; in it they can store more than ten pounds of fish and a pitcher of water ... I have heard it said that one of these birds swallowed a *black baby* a few months old, but could not fly away with it, and so was captured."[vi]

The censor, or interpreter, of the work failed to continue using "Moorish" and dark-complexioned to describe the Mexicans, choosing, in this instance, to use an adjective that was certain and unquestionable—"*black.*"

Just as the librarian had cautioned, the government's account of the Aztecs, written by Cortes, seemed washed, or censored. The African presence was effectively hidden, even while the descriptions exposed the people's braided hair, "Moorish" clothing, their "mosques," "African" police system, and African ornamentation. But now, a *"black baby"* had stood up from the pages. How had the censors missed that?!

The secret that was seeping out of the Spanish records ripped an opening in the veil that had been draped over pre-Columbian history. According to most modern historians, the Aztecs and other Mexicans had walked from Asia, across a vanished Bering Strait land bridge near Alaska, through Canada, then down the western coast of North America to become advanced "Indian" civilizations from one end of the Americas to the other.

I turned back to the writings to see if there was a clear description of Motecuhzoma Not surprisingly, the Spaniards admitted that the Aztec leader was "...a man of middling size, thin, and, like all Indians, of a very dark complexion..."[vii]

Historians have not agreed on a date for the arrival of the Aztecs—or the other Mexicans—into the Valley of Mexico. They have, however, agreed that the Aztecs built their impressive capital city Tenochtitlan, in 1325 AD.

There was another important event that occurred near that date, but it happened thousands of miles from Mexico, across the sea, and in the direction, "...where the sun rises."

Chapter 7

"The Malaku 'key' to the Aztecs"

Before I heard about the Kali or saw *The Five Letters of Cortes*, a young Ethiopian, working to earn her Masters degree, sent African history books to me. Martha Malaku had heard of my interest in early African history during conversations with my wife, who worked with the university's Africa Program.

One of the books the Ethiopian scholar sent contained an account of two trans-Atlantic expeditions launched from Mali, a country in West Africa. Written by Dr. Ivan Van Sertima, a professor at Rutgers who had come from South America, the book included an account of African ships sent across the Atlantic Sea by a Mali king called "Abubakari." The ships were launched toward the Americas nearly 200 years before Columbus went across that same sea.

The two Atlantic Sea crossings by the Mali explorers became more important when I noticed that the "Moorish," "black" Aztecs had arrived at Mexico, in ships, about the same time that Mali sent her ships across the Atlantic.

Van Sertima's book introduced those trans-Atlantic voyages through citations from Basil Davidson's *The Lost Cities of Africa*:

"I asked the [Mali] Sultan Musa how it was that power had come to his hands and he replied: 'We come of a house where royalty is transferred by heritage. The monarch who preceded me would not believe that it was impossible to discover the limits of the neighboring sea. He wished to know. He persisted in his plan. He caused the equipping of two hundred ships and filled them with men, and another such number that were filled with gold, water and food for two years. He said to the commanders: Do not return until you have reached the end of the ocean, or when you have exhausted your food and water.'

"They went away, and their absence was long: none came back, and their absence continued. Then a single ship returned. We asked its captain of their adventures and their news. He replied: 'Sultan, we sailed for a long while until we met with what seemed to be a river with a strong current flowing in the open sea. My ship was last. The others sailed on, but as each of them came to that place they did not come back, nor did they reappear; and I do not know what became of them. As for me, I turned where I was and did not enter that current.'"[viii]

Van Sertima then gave a description of the second expedition sent out by Mali.

"[King Abubakari] abandoned Niani and journeyed with a greater part of his court to the plain at the western edge of Mali, where the first fleet had been fitted out and had disembarked…A vast army of craftsmen, dwarfing the planners and workers of the first expedition, were

37

assembled on that plain…he had a special boat built for himself, with a pempi on the poop deck shaded by the bird-emblazoned parasol. He would commander the new expedition himself, keeping in touch with the captains of the fleet by means of the talking drums. Thus, in 1311 he conferred the power of the regency on his brother, Kankan Musa, on the understanding that Kankan was to assume the throne if, after a reasonable lapse of time, the king did not return. Then one day, dressed in a flowing white robe and a jeweled turban, he took leave of Mali and set out with his fleet down the Senegal, heading west across the Atlantic, never to return. He took his griot and half his history with him."[ix]

From conversations with scholars, there was no knowledge of what happened to the ships or the people sent on those trans-Atlantic expeditions.

It is important to notice that, according to the Aztecs, there was only a short sequence of events between the arrival of the Aztecs and the building of the Aztec city, Tenochtitlan, in 1325:

"The Aztec, or Mexica, were the last of the many nomadic tribes to enter the Valley of Mexico. They…attempted to settle in one or another of the flourishing city-states, but wherever they appeared, they were violently driven away as undesirable foreigners… After a whole series of defeats and humiliations, the Aztecs succeeded in establishing themselves on an island in the lake. … The beginnings of the Aztec capital were very humble. It was founded on a low-lying island so undesirable that other tribes had not bothered to occupy it."[x]

The Mali expeditions and the arrival of the Aztecs occurred close enough in time to consider whether there was a connection between the two events.

The Mali trans-Atlantic voyages became critically important when I remembered that Motecuhzoma had said the Aztecs were "foreigners" who arrived "recently" aboard ships that had come from the direction where "the sun rises." From Mexico, West Africa's Mali was in that same direction as the rising sun.

Spanish writers who saw the Aztecs, and who knew the Moors, had revealed that the Aztecs even wore the same clothing used by the Africans called Moors.

Historians agree that the Aztec capital city, Tenochtitlan, was built about 1325 AD.[xi] That date and a short series of events before 1325 do not exclude the Mali colonists and explorers who launched their two expeditions across the Atlantic Sea toward the Americas sometime between 1300 and 1312.

There was one thing that bothered me about the Abubakari history being the history of the "Moorish" Aztecs. Motecuhzoma stated that "the great lord" of his ancestors came on the first ocean voyage and that this "lord" came again on another trip to take the people back to their homeland. The Abubakari history states that the Mali leader did not come on the first expedition. He came with the second Mali expedition. If Motecuhzoma meant that *a* leader, and not necessarily *the* leader, came with the first group, then there was no disagreement with the history from Mali.

I was aware that facts often lose some of their accuracy over time. Still, this possible discrepancy disturbed me.

A month later, I found the Aztec history that removed the doubt regarding whether the Aztecs had an association with Mali. According to a European friar, the Aztecs named their first colony Malinalco.[xii] It was no coincidence that people on an expedition from Mali would name their first colony *Mali-nalco,* just as it was no coincidence that England named its settlement *"New England,"* or that Spain named its land in America, *"New Spain."*

The relationship between Mali and the Aztecs became clearer when I saw what a translator put in his notes about Mali traditions. Explaining his translation of *Sundiata, an Epic of Old Mali,* the translator wrote:

"I have used this word 'Mandingo' to mean the people who inhabited Mali and their language, and as an adjective to mean anything pertaining to these people. ...

"The inhabitants of Mali call themselves Maninka or Mandinka. Malli and Malinke are the Fulani deformations of the words Manding and Mandinka respectively ... it is not astonishing to find villages in old Mali which have 'Mali' for a name. This name could have formerly been that of a city. In old Mali there is one village called Malikoma..."[xiii]

That explanation gave two valuable pieces of understanding. First, the name "Mali" was used with suffixes by Africans to name cities. That could explain the name "Mali-nalco."

The translator also explained the word, *"Malinke."* I had seen this word while reading Cortes' letters. It was the name applied to the Aztec woman who interpreted the Aztec language for Cortes. The Spaniards gained the Aztec woman upon their arrival in Mesoamerica, and

40

they renamed her "Dona Marina." When Spanish writers attempted to explain why the Aztec people referred to this native interpreter as *"La Malinche,"* the Spaniards reported that it was because the name meant "Marina's captain."[xiv] But the African descendants from Mali, the Aztecs, were simply calling the woman what she was— "the Malinke" meaning "the Mandinka."

Further, since Cortes misrepresented himself as being sent by the ruler of the Aztecs' native homeland, Mali, the Aztecs sometimes sarcastically referred to him as a Mandinka, too, calling him "Malinche," in jest.

The Aztec and Mali histories appeared to point to Mali as the original homeland of the Aztecs, especially when consideration was given to: the dates of the Abubakari expeditions; the date for the building of the Aztec capital city; and the names, Malinalco and Malinche. Even the famed cliff caves of Mali were remembered in the Aztec histories.

But the Aztecs were "foreigners" who had "recently arrived." Now I wanted to know who the earlier people were who had built the ancient cities and pyramids in Mexico.

The Aztecs said they didn't know who built the great pyramids at the old, nearby city called Teotihuacan. So, alongside the apparent Aztec-Mali associations, there stood great stone pyramids, hieroglyphs and other things that seemed to point toward Egypt.

I would have to find the history of the people who arrived before the late arriving Aztecs.

But where could I find an uncensored native history that knew those pyramid builders?

Chapter 8

"Whisper the African"

Most scholars who have studied the Maya and Aztec refuse to tell us that the Aztecs arrived on the eastern shore of Mexico, in ships. That history of arrival came directly from the Aztecs so you would think it would be important to publicize that.

I had never heard a scholar explain their silence about the trans-Atlantic origins of the Aztecs. But a leading Mayanist confessed to me that no historian of the Maya, "who values their reputation and career," will admit Africans were in the Americas before Columbus arrived.

Hiding the pre-Columbian presence of Africans was not a new deceit. From the time the Spaniards arrived in Mexico, official efforts to erase the African presence were pursued with a vengeance. Historian William Prescott documented the erasing of the Africans:

"[Their] manuscripts were made of different materials...but for the most part, of a fine fabric from the leaves of the aloe, *agave Americana,* called by the natives, maguey, which grows luxuriantly over the tablelands of Mexico. A sort of paper was made from it, resembling somewhat the Egyptian papyrus...

"At the time of the arrival of the Spaniards, great quantities of these manuscripts were treasured up in the country...The first archbishop of Mexico, Don Juan de

Zumarraga...collected these paintings from every quarter, especially from Tezcuco, the most cultivated capital in Anahuac, and the great depository of the national archives. He then caused them to be piled up in a 'mountain-heap,'—as it is called by the Spanish writers themselves—in the market-place of Tlateloco, and reduced them all to ashes!

"The unlettered soldiers were not slow in imitating the example of their prelate. Every chart and volume which fell into their hands was wantonly destroyed..."[xv]

But destroying the books and paintings was not sufficient to erase the forbidden histories of the Americas. Records had also been carved, painted, and otherwise depicted, on monuments, including temples that resembled hieroglyphics-covered temples that ancient Egypt built in northeast Africa.

Spain attacked the images on the temples in Mexico. Even the image of Motecuhzoma was erased from history. Prescott wrote:

"They demolished, in a short time, all the Aztec temples, great and small, so that not a vestige of them remained."[xvi]

"Sculptured images were so numerous, that the foundations of the cathedral in the *plaza mayor*, the great square of Mexico, are said to be entirely composed of them. This spot may, indeed, be regarded as the Aztec forum,--the great depository of the treasures of ancient sculpture, which now lie hid in its bosom. Such monuments are spread all over the capital, however, and a new cellar can hardly be dug, or foundation laid, without turning up some of the mouldering relics of barbaric art. But they are little heeded, and, if not wantonly broken in pieces at once, are usually worked into the rising wall, or supports of the new edifice. Two celebrated bas-reliefs, of the last Montezuma and his father, cut in the solid rock, in the beautiful groves of Chapoltepec, were deliberately destroyed, as late as the last century, by order of the government!"[xvii]

One morning it dawned on me that Mexico is still governed by a people who arrived from Spain. Maybe Mayanists and other historians have no choice but to censure, censor, and erase the pre-Columbian African presence. But that is not certain.

What *is* certain is that scholars who want to work at pre-Columbian ruins in Mexico, Central America and South America often must get permission from Hispanic administrators in those countries. If there were some agreement between those governments to hide the history of the Africans, then what could their motive be?

If there was no motive to deny the pre-Columbian African presence, why would a university professor deny an African presence in pre-Columbian America then whisper in notes at the back of his published book that rulers of some of the most important Maya nations called themselves *"black rulers"*? [xviii]

So whispered a Mayanist.

Chapter 9

"*Europe called it* The Black Legend"

I was awestruck when I saw how Cortes and his group marched into the Aztecs' capital city, right into the middle of the Aztec strength! As I continued to read the accounts, my wonder became flooded with hatred. The chroniclers began describing how the Spaniards butchered women, men and children; or how they burned some elderly man, while he was alive—all to uncover some piece of gold!

It was not an insult to my senses alone. When the barbarous cruelty and gluttonous behavior of the Spanish soldiers were publicized, people throughout Europe began to scorn the name of Spain. The murderous expeditions became known around Europe as "*the Black Legend.*"

During a conversation with Motecuhzoma, in the Aztec palace, Cortes and his soldiers suddenly attacked this ruler, chained him, and threatened to kill him if he did not send messengers to bring gold. Then the Spaniards slaughtered a group of unarmed Aztecs, to get the gold ornaments that adorned those celebrants, who were performing religious ceremonies in the city.

When news of these murders spread through the Aztec communities, the Africans called Aztecs launched an impassioned attack against the Aztec palace where the Spaniards had fortified themselves. The attack was so fierce and fearful that Cortes was forced to abandon his kidnapping schemes against important Aztec dignitaries. According to one Aztec account, after threatening Motecuhzoma, to discover his private treasuries of gold, the Spaniards then murdered him.

When night came, Cortes and his marauders attempted to sneak out of the city. A woman saw them and shouted out the alarm. During the fearful chase that followed, the Spaniards left gold, horses, soldiers, and anything else that slowed their flight from the city.

Cortes and, according to some writers, only half his army, escaped to the coast and waited there until more guns, cannons and soldiers arrived.

Months later, Cortes led a second attack against the Aztec capital. This time, blasts from Spanish cannons leveled the wonder-filled city, and over 240,000 Mexicans were massacred. So went part of the barbarous events called *the Black Legend.*

Following the fall of the Aztec capital city, thousands of Mexican men, women, and even children, were burned alive, decapitated, hung, or otherwise killed for failure to give gold to the Spaniards. Other Mexicans were chained and sent to Cuba as slaves.

After the invasion and destruction of the Aztec empire, Spain immediately began sending Spanish people into Mexico. In time, many of these Spanish colonists assumed the name of the conquered people, calling themselves, Mexicans.

Aware of the difference between the two groups of "Mexicans," some writers from Mexico show their enlightenment by referring to the original Mexicans as "pre-Hispanic" Mexicans. Knowledgeable Hispanic writers even ridiculed the famous Spanish army commander Santa Anna for claiming the heritage of the Black Mexicans who battled Cortes.

Into the genocide of *the Black Legend* stepped the Franciscan friar, Bernardino de Sahagun.

At the start of the search, the Special Collections librarian had told me Sahagun was "*the* authority" on pre-Hispanic Mexico.

Chapter 10

"Silencing Sahagun's Forbidden Histories*"*

Fray Sahagun arrived two years after the destruction of the Aztec capital city. While befriending Aztecs and other Mexicans who had survived the Black Legend, Sahagun learned that Spain had attempted to destroy, or confiscate, every Aztec book and written record that could be found.

Sahagun set out to reconstruct those records. He convinced the Mexicans of his sincerity in re-establishing the record of their histories. Eventually, the Mexicans granted personal interviews to Sahagun. Then, they brought writings and drawings that had escaped the mass destruction ordered by Spain and its church.

In an extraordinary footnote in Prescott's *History of the Conquest of Mexico* is a detailed account of Sahagun's efforts to recover the pre-Columbian histories of the Americas:

"The most important authority...wherever the Aztec religion is concerned, is Bernardino de Sahagun, a Franciscan friar, contemporary with the Conquest. His great work, *Historia Universal de Nueva Espa* has been recently printed for the first time. The circumstances attending its compilation and subsequent fate form one of the most remarkable passages in literary history.

"The work presented a mass of curious information, that attracted much attention among his brethen...Sahagun had views more liberal than those of his order, whose blind zeal would willingly have annihilated every monument of art and human ingenuity, which had not been produced under the influence of Christianity. They refused to allow him the necessary aid to transcribe his papers, which he had been so many years in preparing, under the pretext that the expense was too great for their order to incur...What was worse, his provincial got possession of his manuscripts, which were soon scattered among the different religious houses in the country.

"In this forlorn state of his affairs, Sahagun drew up a brief statement of the nature and contents of his work, and forwarded it to Madrid. It fell into the hands of Don Juan de Ovando, president of the Council for the Indies, who was so much interested in it, that he ordered the manuscripts to be restored to their author, with the request that he would at once set about translating them into Castillian. This was accordingly done. His papers were recovered, though not without the menace of *ecclesiastical censures*; and the octogenarian author began the work of translation from the Mexican, in which they had been originally written by him thirty years before...

"...It was sent to Madrid. There seemed now to be no further reason for postponing its publication, the importance of which could not be doubted. But from this moment it disappears; and we hear nothing further of it, for more than two centuries, except only as a valuable work, which had once existed, and was probably buried in some one of the numerous cemeteries of learning in which Spain abounds.

"At length, toward the close of the last century, the indefatigable Munoz succeeded in disinterring the long lost manuscript from the place tradition had assigned to it—the library of a convent at Tolosa, in Navarre, the northern extremity of Spain...Thus this remarkable work, which was denied the honors of the press during the author's lifetime, after passing into oblivion, re-appeared, at the distance of nearly three centuries, not in his own country, but in foreign lands widely remote from each other...The hieroglyphical paintings, which accompanied the text, are...missing.

"...Sahagun produced several other works, of a religious or philological character. Some of these were voluminous, but none have been printed."[xix]

After hearing how the government confiscated, censured, then hid the histories compiled by Sahagun, I was anxious to see the version of the work that finally surfaced.

Before I could delve into the work of Sahagun, a professor at my university telephoned me. He said he had been told of my interest in the Aztecs. He advised me to quit the search and showed me the account that, he assured me, would make me understand that the origin of the Aztecs was in North America. He named a Spanish writer called Duran — whom I was familiar with — as the source of the history that would convince me to end my search.

So, now I share the Duran explanation, which suggests that the original homeland of the Aztecs was in North America, north of Mexico.

"The only knowledge of their origins that I have obtained from my Indian informants tells of the seven caves where their ancestors dwelt for so long and which they abandoned in order to seek this land, some coming first and others later until these caves were totally deserted. The caves are in Teocolhuacan, which is also called Aztlan, "Land of Herons," which we are told is found toward the north and near the region of La Florida. ... "[xx]

That explanation appeared to create a dilemma between Motecuhzoma's own claim that the Aztecs came from across the sea in the direction "...of the rising sun," and Duran's history, which brings the Aztecs from the north, out of a place called "La Florida." Historians explained that "La Florida" was a large region that stretched across what is now the southern United States.

The dilemma about the two directions of origin seemed important until the Sahagun histories solved the problem. Regarding the arrival of the 'Mexicans' into the land now called Mexico, Sahagun recorded:

"Here is the account that the elders used to pronounce: at a certain time which no one can speak of any more, that today no one can remember, those who came here to sow the grandfathers, the grandmothers....*They came in many groups in their boats on the water, and there they arrived at the edge of the water, on the northern coast, and there where their boats remained is called*

Panutla, which means where one passes over the water, today it is called Pantla (Panuco). Subsequently they followed the shoreline, they went in search of the mountains, some the white mountains and mountains that smoke, they approached Quauhtemallan, following the shoreline....

"Afterwards they came, they arrived at the place called Tamoanchan, which means 'we are looking for our home.'

"And once they had been in Tamoanchan for some time, they then moved on, left the land, to others they left it, those that are called Olmecas . . ."[xxi]

" 'The different Nahua peoples are also *called Chichimecs because they returned* coming from the Chichimec land; it is said that they returned from Chicomoztoc.... But the people from the direction of the face of the Sun are not called Chichimecs, they are called Olmecas . . . '"[xxii]

Sahagun's *Forbidden Histories* showed there was no contradiction between what Motecuhzoma had said and what Duran's Mexican informants had reported to him. All the "Nahua" people arrived in ships at Panutla—on the eastern seashore of Mexico—and they had come from the direction of the rising sun. The ships left and followed the shoreline until they reached Guatemala (*"Quauhtemallan"*). Then the people returned to Mexico, where a group remained in that region and was eventually given the name "Olmec." Other groups left that place, and went northward into the North American region called by Duran, "La Florida." When these groups returned to Mexico from their explorations in the North, they were given the name Chichimec, meaning "returning."

Duran's account had picked up the history where some of the people were returning from the North.

It may be true that some group, or groups, of people immigrated into the North American continent using some lost Bering Strait land bridge, but the Aztecs, and Olmecs were not those people.

Scholars say the Olmecs arrived at Mexico more than 3,000 years ago. So, Sahagun had recovered forbidden histories that were much older than the Aztec civilization. Sahagun had reached into the era of ancient Egypt and the Old Testament.

Interestingly, Sahagun's *Forbidden Histories* showed that the people who arrived at Panutla carried books written with red and black hieroglyphics—inventions uniquely identified with ancient Egypt.

Most importantly, Sahagun's histories provided the *written* record of a foreign arrival from the direction of Africa that many early historians—and most modern scholars—have claimed does not exist.

These ancient immigrants did not arrive on the western coast of Mexico, as you would have expected if they had come from the Orient, as scholars claim. Sahagun found that the Mexicans, like the Aztecs, arrived at the eastern coast of Mexico ... in ships!

I noticed another extraordinary thing in the *Forbidden Histories*: the people arriving in their ships, at the eastern seashore of Mexico, carrying books of red and black hieroglyphs, were called "Nahual people." It didn't escape my perception that this name could mean *Nile*.

Chapter 11

"The Pharaoh and a man named Meci"

Sahagun's *Forbidden Histories* provided the names of two men who came with the Olmec ships to Mexico. One of these men, "Meci," may be the reason the land was called "Meci-co" and the people, "Meci-cans." Three thousand years later we still call the land "Mexico" and its people, "Mexicans."

No less important was the other leader, "Nahuaque." In ancient Egypt there had lived a Pharaoh named Taharque. The similarity between Nahuaque and Taharque was too curious to ignore, especially since these ships arrived at Mexico with books written with red and black hieroglyphs. Pharaoh Taharque's Egypt wrote with red and black hieroglyphs, too.

One scholar suggested that it should have concerned me that "Nahuaque" was not spelled exactly like the name "Taharque." It didn't matter that the names were not exactly alike. Ancient names often lost parts of their original sounds over time. According to the German Egyptologist Henrich Brugsch-Bey, history had recorded events about Pharaoh Taharque using widely varying names for him. Brugsch explained:

"He is well known in antiquity as a conqueror. In the Bible he appears under the name of Tirhakah; in the classic writers as Tearko, Etearchus, Tarakus, and Tarkus: the Egyptian inscriptions know him simply as the lord of Kamit, Tesherit, and Kipkip—i.e. Egypt, the red land, and Ethiopia."[xxiii]

My search turned toward Egypt to find histories that knew Pharaoh Taharque.

A stone called the Serapeum Stele recorded an event that happened at the end of Taharka's reign.

"Year 24, fourth month of the second season (eighth month), day 23, under the majesty of the King of Upper and Lower Egypt, Taharka, living forever.

"The god was conducted in peace *to the beautiful West...*"

Priests had accompanied Taharka to "the beautiful West."

Modern scholars responded that "the West" was simply an Egyptian term for a region on the west bank of the Nile River, in northeast Africa.

If I had not been familiar with Sahagun's *Forbidden Histories*, Taharka's trip to the "beautiful West" might not have stirred any excitement within me. However, I had digested Sahagun's account and I suspected that Taharka had died and the Egyptian priests were taking him to the "beautiful West"—to America—for burial. I knew that the description, "beautiful West," could never be a description of the bare, torn hills and caves on the western side of the Nile River.

I was not sure where, in the Americas, Taharka was taken for burial, but there was one city that seemed a good candidate. The Aztecs said the ancient, ruined city in Mexico known as Teotihuacan had been a burial place for rulers who died and became gods. Throughout Teotihuacan stood terraced bases that were once surmounted with pyramids, temples, and monuments built to honor deceased "gods."

Mexicans told Sahagun that the long, wide street in Teotihuacan was called the *"Street of the Dead"* and *"The Road of the Gods."* They informed Sahagun that Teotihuacan was an ancient city and they said of this burial center:

"And so they named it Teotihuacan:
because it was the burial place of rulers.
For it is said: When we die,
we do not truly die,
because we are alive,
because we are brought back to life,
because we still live,
because we awaken....
Thus, the elders said:
"He who died became a god."[xxiv]

I turned back to the Egyptian stele. The writing stated that Nahuaque was a *"god"* who was "conducted in peace to the beautiful West." That inscription mentions the 24th year of Taharka's reign. There had been no inscription found that records a 25th year of reign for Taharka.

Likewise, the Sahagun history never states that Nahuaque *does* anything; nor does Nahuaque even speak. The priests said that they speak for him. That is exactly what we could expect if this leader were dead and being transported to a burial place.

According to the Scriptures, during the time of Taharque, Persians attacked Jerusalem and enslaved its people. The Greeks wrote that the city, Thebes, was also enslaved while Taharque was ruling Egypt. The enslavement of Jerusalem and Thebes at the same time would eventually prove to be more than a coincidence.

Three avenues were before me. I could attempt to find more Egyptian writings that defined "the beautiful West"; I could search for more Egyptian records about Taharka; or I could search Egyptian hieroglyphs for *any* ships going to "the West."

Anticipation stirred my adrenaline when I saw the meaning of Egyptian hieroglyphs on an ancient, inscribed stone called the Tanis Stele. This stele clarified that "the West" did not refer to the west bank of the Nile River. The inscriptions extended the meaning of "the West" far away, to a land where the sun sets.

A scribe, writing for Pharaoh Taharque, wrote:

"My father, Amon, promised to me to place all lands under my feet [*missing text*] the east as far as the rising of Re, and the west as far as his setting."

"*Re*" was a name given to an ancient Egyptian ruler whom priests honored by allowing the sun to be a symbol of him—because both the man, "Re," and the sun had provided great benefits to the Egyptian people.

The Tanis Stele explained that Taharka had ruled lands as far as the setting of the sun, in the West. The same stele declared that Taharka had been away from home for many years on some expedition, beginning at age twenty.

Other ancient Egyptian records described building projects carried out during the reign of Taharka. One of these inscriptions mentioned something very curious—pyramids that had tall "stairways," which led to temples on top of the pyramids!

I had seen ancient pyramids in the Americas and I knew that most of these pyramids had tall stairways.

The pyramids in what we now call Egypt, in northeast Africa, have no stairways on their exteriors or temples on their summits!

The ancient Egyptian hieroglyphs were describing pyramids in the Americas, not the pyramids in northeastern Africa!

I began looking for inscriptions that described staircases on Egyptian pyramids. Then I remembered something that would narrow the search. There are pyramids in the Americas that have two staircases that reach to their summits. If I could find Egyptian inscriptions that mentioned pyramids with double-staircases, the search could possibly begin to match American pyramids to events in the Egyptian histories.

For weeks, nothing appeared. Then, at one o'clock in the morning, a double-staircase inscription came into view. The Egyptian account of the double stairway is on a stele reportedly taken from a temple on the Nile River. The stele speaks of blessings granted to Ramses II by an Egyptian deity. Here is the *"double staircase"* inscription carved on the stele:

"Thou hast made an august residence, to make strong the boundary of the Two Lands: [it is] plentiful in provisions for Egypt, flourishing like the four pillars of heaven…I put on thy crown with my own two hands, when thou appearest upon *the great double staircase.*" [xxv]

A large pyramid with a great double staircase had stood in the Aztec capital city when the conquistadors arrived in Mexico. Because of something I knew about this island, I thought the double staircase mentioned on the stele was referring to the large pyramid on the Aztec island. But that was not the right pyramid.

Another pyramid, the greatest pyramid in the Americas, had the "*great* double staircase." That stairway is on the Pyramid of the Sun at Teotihuacan.

Was the Egyptian stele revealing that Rameses had been crowned Pharaoh on the double staircase of a pyramid ... in Mexico?

Chapter 12

"No ear for the common tongue"

I had located ancient Egyptian histories that seemed to provide a written record of Egypt's knowledge of "the West" and the Americas. A "great double staircase" had provided a pathway to the discovery.

Several weeks after sending some of the findings to Princeton University for review and criticism, I saw a centuries-old illustration that depicted black-skinned Aztecs meeting Cortes when he arrived at the Aztec capital. The illustration was published in 1724 on a front page of Antonio de Solis' *History of the Conquest of Mexico*. The artist had allowed the buildings in the illustration to be Moorish in design, and he had allowed all but one of the Aztecs to be black-skinned. He, or someone, had lightened, considerably, the complexion of Motecuhzoma.

With so keen an understanding about the Aztec buildings being Moorish in design, the artist should have been familiar with the conquistadors' other descriptions, which said Motecuhzoma was, "...a man of middling size, thin, and ... of a very dark complexion."

I telephoned the professor at Princeton who had sent me a courteous response about the Aztec findings. He had written, "I hope that you have success in publishing it for it deserves a public hearing and critical discussion … [but] I don't think the color issue is persuasive."

An early copy of Solis' book, showing the Black Aztecs, was in the Rare Books Library at Princeton. I sent a note to the professor, urging him to see the historical illustration of the Black Aztecs at his university.

I had assumed that the Spaniards' clear descriptions of the Aztecs, including the description, "black baby," would bring the true African image of the Aztecs into view. I was wrong. There was a mental blockage, even within the imaginations of many African Americans.

Beyond the Solis illustration, I had seen pre-Columbian images of the Aztecs, and the Aztecs had painted themselves as black-skinned Africans. I had seen the famed, ancient, Olmec stone heads from Mexico that showed African features on these original Mexicans who had followed Meci. I had seen the pre-Columbian images of the Aztec deities, with their Black African features.

I had failed to consider that the Spaniards' written descriptions of the Aztecs as Africans would not be strong enough to erase the straight-haired images of "Indians" painted in modern imaginations about the Aztecs.

How could I get these "Forbidden Histories" known?

I gathered the discoveries, pored over them to determine the clearest discoveries, and then I called the local newspaper, the *Fort Worth Star Telegram*, and asked for the editorial writer who spoke with me occasionally.

I didn't know him personally, nor even well enough to guess how he would react to this kind of news. He had impressed me as being intelligent and able to make unbiased judgments from facts, and he was African-American.

"You have what?" He queried, more as a punctuation of astonishment than as a question. "If you have what you say you have, that will need something bigger than my column. Let me talk to someone on the news desk."

He paused. I tried to imagine the questions that were going through his mind. There was no way that I could prove the discovery in a short phone call. Which single piece of proof could I give that would convince someone of what I had found? Before I could assemble an answer to my question, the writer's voice vibrated through the receiver.

"That's an awesome discovery if that pans out," he said, more serious than before.

His voice was not encouraging. I felt anxiety rising because of his words. He said something else that I do not remember, and then he hung up, leaving me wondering whether another phone call would come.

After a day passed with no phone call from the *Star Telegram*, I telephoned Phil Record. Record's age and experience had settled him into an executive public relations position with the newspaper. He had met me twenty years earlier, when he recruited me for a journalism scholarship awarded by his newspaper.

Record informed me that he was no longer in a position to make decisions regarding which stories would be printed, but he told me that he would talk with one of the editors.

Two days later, a *Star Telegram* writer called me. He wanted to know if anyone "reputable" had seen the findings. "Has anybody like a professor or somebody knowledgeable in history seen your work?" He asked.

My memory came alive. One of the administrators at the university where I worked had given the same query. She said nothing would happen with the findings unless I found someone "with a Ph.D." to argue for the discovery.

"Who are you?" She had mocked. "You are nobody. You don't have a Ph.D. in the field. Nobody will give you the time of day."

I thought she was being snobbish. I knew she had a doctorate degree—or Ph.D.—in a field unrelated to history. I decided that she just didn't know the extent of the proof that existed for the discoveries. I was sure everybody would want to know this!

Months later, I would realize how wrong I was.

The reporter's voice slapped me back to reality. "You call me back when you have someone with knowledge about that subject—someone who is ready to support what you are saying."

The reporter did not appear to be biased one way or the other about the discoveries.

I had refused to give the deepest details about the findings to the scholars, because I reasoned that something this important and historic would be too great a temptation for theft.

The reporter's comment made me reconsider giving up the discoveries, fully.

Chapter 13

"If these should hold their peace . . ."

He had his doctorate and was a scholar of pre-Columbian history at the university where I worked. After a long wait, he finally arrived at his office as I was leaving. His glance at the clock on the wall warned me to make it fast, so I blurted it out.

"I've found the records showing the Aztecs who met Cortes in 1519 were probably Africans."

A smirk curved at the corners of his mouth, but I continued.

"Cortes, his secretary, and Castillo—one of his officers—described Motecuhzoma as being very dark-complexioned. They wrote that the nation of people they found here was of the same complexion."

"That doesn't mean black," he countered. "To the Europeans, of course they were considered dark complexioned. But they were just copper toned in skin color."

Then he offered the name of some books that could help me remove my misunderstandings.

"I've already read those," I quickly responded, noticing that it was now 5 o'clock. I had not offered the most convincing discovery. I let it out.

"The writings of Sahagun say the Mexicans did not come from the north or northwest into Mexico. Sahagun wrote that they arrived by boat, coming from the direction of the rising sun, and that they landed on the Gulf Coast of Mexico at Panutla. Even Motecuhzoma told Cortes that the Aztecs were not from this land, but were newcomers and foreigners who arrived by boat, coming from a land that lay in the direction of Africa. These black Aztecs, wearing clothing described as African in design, were in fact, Africans."

He looked away from the papers that I offered to him.

"I think you've misunderstood something in the writings," he calmly insulted. "I've got to go. I hope you'll keep me posted on your work."

His secretary was standing at her desk by the door, ready to lock up for the evening. I thanked him for his time and gathered up my papers.

I was almost through the large, clear, glass doors when I turned to face this "doctor."

"The Spanish explorers did not say the Aztecs were brown, or copper-toned, they said black, and very dark. They *were* Africans."

I was not prodding for a response. I wanted him to know that his feeble denials had absolutely no effect on my perceptions. By now, I had consulted over a dozen of the most knowledgeable historians on Aztec and Mexica history. I had absorbed Sahagun, Diego Duran, Castillo, Columbus, and much of the encyclopedic work of Hubert Bancroft. My confidence in the African presence in ancient America could not be easily rattled. I was already armed with the texts that the professors wanted to use to deny the African presence. I knew those texts argued for—*not against*—the Africans.

The next day I telephoned the research librarian who had introduced me to the Black Caribs, at the start of the search.

Her response caught me with my naiveté up. When I told her that I had found that the Aztecs and other Mexicans were Blacks and that they pointed toward Africa as their land of origin, there was absolutely no response from her. Finally, she interrupted the silence to say that she had to go. Then she hung up the phone.

She had been so exuberant about her knowledge of the Black people who lived in the "New World" when Columbus arrived. Now, there was no emotion. What had happened?

I was going through the paces at work, when it suddenly dawned on me what had probably occurred with the librarian. I had forgotten that she was a post-Hispanic Mexican and was probably descended from Spaniards. Maybe it was exciting for her to upset *other* European history, but now I had found Blacks in Mexico, and maybe that was unacceptable. Maybe Mexican history was not to be touched.

Later, I saw in my notes that she had not allowed Blacks to be in Mexico. She had said to me, "I know there were several groups of Blacks here, and not just in the islands, but in South America, too."

I shrugged it off.

A thought kept drifting through my head. It was something from the Bible about stones crying out. I found the passage in the 19th chapter of *Luke*:

"And when he was come nigh, even now at the descent of the Mount of Olives, the whole multitude of the disciples began to rejoice and praise God with a loud voice for all the mighty works that they had seen;

"Saying, Blessed be the King that cometh in the name of the Lord: peace in heaven, and glory in the highest.

"And some of the Pharisees from among the multitude said unto him, Master, rebuke thy disciples.

"And he answered and said unto them, I tell you that, if these should hold their peace, the stones would immediately cry out."

When I talked with my wife about my belief that God was giving some special thought to our house, she threw her gaze against me, to measure me for sanity.

"I don't know if you should put that in the writing," she advised. "I think that would take away from the seriousness of what you're saying."

"Things that I didn't know existed are falling into my lap," I said. "And I understand them, even when scholars don't seem to know what they mean."

"I understand what you're saying," she offered, "but still, people are going to see it as though you're painting yourself to be some kind of super-human, and that's going to take away from the work."

It would be years before I realized how powerfully unerring her words were. She saw what I couldn't see. In my blindness, I rushed to find the rocks.

Chapter 14

"Then came Bentresh"

While searching through ancient Egyptian records, I noticed the story of a woman whose name seemed to be *"Bentresh."* The stone with her history may now be in Paris at the Bibliotheque Nationale Museum, but the story is also cut into an ancient temple called Abu Simbel, in northeast Africa.

According to the Bentresh inscriptions, a foreign chief in a place called "the Two Lands" offered his daughter to Ramses for marriage. Ramses married the girl and took her back to Egypt. Some time after the marriage, the foreign chief came from his kingdom—called both Kheta and Beken—to meet with Ramses. The Kheta chief asked Ramses to send a physician to heal one of the chief's other daughters, Bentresh, who seemed to be "possessed with a demonic spirit."

An Egyptian physician was sent from Egypt to Beken. Unable to heal the girl, the physician returned to Egypt then went again to Beken with a religious idol. After the girl was healed, the physician and the idol returned to Egypt.

The fact that it took, consistently, 17 months of travel to reach Beken was one of the most astonishing revelations in the Bentresh inscriptions. Egyptologists who saw the Bentresh account attempted to explain away the incredible 17-month voyages by arguing that the Egyptian priests who had ordered the inscriptions to be carved had erred in their facts. It was the height of arrogance that historians continued to apply that explanation to Egyptian hieroglyphic accounts that did not agree with the historians' ideas about the past.

Egyptologist Henry Breasted added several footnotes to the Bentresh account about the 17-month-long voyages. Two of his footnotes confirm the consistent 17-month of travel needed to travel from Egypt to the city in the "Two Lands" called both Beken and Bekhten.

"As the god later consumes one year and five months in going to Bekhten, the round trip between Egypt and Bekhten should take some thirty-four months. This exactly suits the ... passage, according to which the returning wise man has been absent nearly three years, which allows for a short stay in Bekhten."[xxxvi]

And:

"The round trip consumed 34 months (1 year and 5 months each way), and he had remained in Bekhten 45 months, a total absence of 79 months, or 6 years and 7 months. As he left Egypt in the ninth month of the year 26, if that date be late in the year 26, an absence of 6 years and 7 months would put his return in the year 33, as the priestly author of the inscription has done."[xxxvii]

There was no mistake, it required 17 months to reach Bekhten (Beken) from Egypt, and also 17 months to return. Breasted, Brugsch and other Egyptologists announced that they never located Bekhten.

In other Egyptian records, the people of Bekhten were called "the Beken," and "the Bekhen."

The ancient writings placed Beken in "the Two Lands," which the inscriptions also called "the Northland and the Southland."

Because scholars had interpreted "the Two Lands" to mean Egypt along the Nile, they were at a lost to explain why it required, consistently, 17 months of travel between Beken from Egypt.

On this riddle called Bekhen, Brugsch wrote:

"It is difficult to say where the land of Bakhtan (sic) should be sought. A journey of seventeen months from (Luxor, Egypt) to the foreign city shows that it was very distant. The ... stay of Ra-messu XII. in the river-land of Naharain suggests a Syrian town."[xxviii]

The problem with the suggestion that Beken was in Syria was that Syria was not thought by the Egyptologists to be in "the Two Lands," and of course it does not take 17 months of sailing to reach the place now called Syria, from the place now called Egypt on the Nile.

Several weeks after learning of Bentresh, I saw scenes about the Bentresh history carved on an ancient ball court in Mexico, at the Olmec city called Tajin.

In one scene, an Egyptian priest uses a tapered stone to undo the demonic possession of the woman. The Egyptian narrative about Bentresh explains that a magic talisman stone was used to help remove the demonic spirit from the princess.[xxix]

Unfamiliar with the meaning of the Tajin scenes, modern historians said that the woman is being sacrificed. The historians saw the priest standing above the woman, holding the tapered talisman stone, and they incorrectly deduced that the stone is about to be plunged into the chest of the woman.

70

But Tajin was not Beken, or was it? Several months later, I saw a map that showed the ancient Maya city called *Becan,* on the Yucatan Peninsula.

Now it could be understood why it took 17 months to reach Bekhen from the city where Ramses was, in northeast Africa.

Had the mysterious Beken of the Egyptian histories been found that easily?

Probably so, according to the buildings found in Becan and Egyptian descriptions of the buildings at Beken.

The Becan of the Yucatan matched the distinguishing marks given by the Egyptian hieroglyphs about the Beken that Ramses knew.

After locating Beken in the Yucatan, another Egyptian record appeared which firmed up the belief that the American Becan was the Beken of Ramses. In a well-published ancient Egyptian papyrus called "The Report of Wenamon," the names of several important Maya cities near Becan are given, including *"...Dor, a city of Thekel..."*ˣˣˣ

Modern scholars have published that the ancient Yucatan city called *Mira-Dor* was indeed a city ruled by the nearby greater Mayan city called *Tikal.*

With ancient Egyptian records about 17-month-long voyages to reach Bekhen, with an ancient American city called Becan, and with carvings at an ancient city in Mexico portraying events about the famed cure of a Beken princess, the Bentresh Stele became too overwhelming for the scholars to ignore. The senior historian for the *National Geographic* magazine wrote that the Bentresh Stela and Becan were the most critical findings of the discoveries I had sent to him.

Bekhen was fascinating, but my attention was moving toward another Egyptian city called Memphis.

Something kept telling me that the Egyptian capital city, Memphis, had been built on an island in Mexico. But each time I attempted to investigate that belief, some stone would pull me in another direction.

When the senior historian for *National Geographic* magazine agreed to write a review for a part of the findings, the search for Memphis could wait no longer.

Chapter 15

"World's largest city has completely 'vanished'"

Sometimes, fate has a way of overruling your best laid plans.

While gathering ancient records about Memphis, I saw something about another city that overwhelmed my senses. I could not believe what I was seeing!

An ancient 'map' showing the largest city ever built by ancient Egypt lay before my eyes. Egypt had built the city in Mexico!

I looked at the descriptions, which provided a sort of 'map.' While following the conquistadors' movements across Mexico, I had seen this city. I knew where it was!

Now, in my hands was the ancient 'map' of this city. The descriptions were so unique that only one city in the world would match them. I pored over the descriptions of Egypt's Heliopolis, again. I wanted to be absolutely sure.

Ancient descriptions of the famed Heliopolis reveal that this 17,000-year-old burial center was a city with: at least two great pyramids; enough burial temples and pyramids to house several thousand years of Egyptian rulers, priests and dignitaries, and; another Wonder of the Ancient World, called "the Labyrinth," which had at least 3,000 burial chambers.

The descriptions, more than 2,000 years old, describe a ceremonial boulevard at Heliopolis that was so large, so wide, and so *deep* that one Greek historian wrote of this extraordinary road:

"For ten years the people were afflicted in making the road whereon the stones were dragged, the making of which road was to my thinking a task but a little lighter than the building of the (Great Pyramid), for the road is five furlongs long and ten fathoms broad, and raised at its highest to a height of eight fathoms, and it is all of stone polished and carven with figures."[xxxi]

The historian wrote that this monumental road ascended to a hill where the two "Great Pyramids" of Egypt stood within two man-made pools of water.

Further, the old writings revealed that beside these Great Pyramids sprawled the Labyrinth—with 1,500 rooms above ground and 1,500 burial chambers below those.

There was more. Near to the Labyrinth, the Great Pyramids, and the monumental road would be a man-made "sea" so amazingly constructed that it was admired as one of the Seven Wonders of the Ancient World:

"…more marvellous (than the Labyrinth) is the lake Moeris, by which it stands. This lake has a circuit of three thousand six hundred furlongs….Its length is from north to south; the deepest part has a depth of fifty fathoms."[xxxii]

" … Sometimes it is called *She*, i.e., 'basin' or 'lake'; sometimes *She-uer*, 'the great lake basin,' or, *Mi-uer*, 'the great lake.' From the most usual designation, *She*, the country was called *Ta-She*, 'the land of the lake' ..." [xxxiii]

When I saw this 'map' of Heliopolis, I knew it was pointing to a city whose pyramids and ruins are still sprawled across the Highland Plateau of Mexico.

Chapter 16

"Pharaohs' burial grounds found in Mexico"

At Teotihuacan, ancient descriptions of Heliopolis are matched marvel-for-marvel, including: a "great" road that was originally a half-mile long;[xxxiv] a wondrous Labyrinth with over 1,500 rooms above-ground;[xxxv] two Great Pyramids standing in stone-lined depressions that were once manmade pools; and nearby, a great manmade lake with the pre-Columbian name "Texcoco" (but pronounced "TESHE-KO-KO"). Here was the famed lake region called *"Ta-She"* that ancient writers had said was near Heliopolis.

It was the unmistakable presence of Egypt's Great Pyramids at Teotihuacan, Mexico that unlocked the *"Forbidden Histories"* and the secret locations of Egypt's cities in the Americas.

The city's name, "Teotihuacan," probably refers back to the most ancient era of Egypt. It was at Heliopolis that the Egyptian deity called "Tehuti" (Thoth) judged the souls of the deceased:

"Frequent mention is made in the old records of the royal gods, as of real personages. Besides the name of their dynasty they have a second name of honour, and, just like the Pharaohs, they bear respectively the authentic title under which the god Tehuti, the sacred scribe of the gods, registered each of them in the 'Book of the Kings,' at the command of the Sun god, Ra. They have their individual history, which the scribes wrote down in the temple books..."[xxxvi]

When I shared with the scholars that the pyramids at Teotihuacan were the famed *Great Pyramids*, they took me for a fool and slowly pointed out to me—always with a smile—that my work must be a simple error of a simple mind, because the Great Pyramids could very easily be seen standing along the Nile in northeast Africa.

I took no great joy in their misery when I pulled out a small green book and pointed to this single ancient description of one of the Great Pyramids:

"This pyramid was made like a stairway with tiers, or steps."![xxxvii]

That simple description, alone, destroyed the scholars' argument that the pyramids in northeast Africa were the Great Pyramids called Wonders of the World. That description of the Great Pyramids as enormous, *stepped* pyramids came from Herodotus, who had seen the Great Pyramids. He described them as being built in a tiered design, and the two Great Pyramids at Teotihuacan showed that tier design. The two great pyramids in Africa are smooth-sided and have no tiers!

The scholars I showed the description to were so discomforted by the "tier" description that some excuse always—and suddenly—surface, to end the meeting. There was never an opportunity to show the remaining descriptions that placed, on the exterior of the Great

Pyramids, broad staircases that reached temples which stood on the summits of the Great Pyramids. Of course, the so-called "Great Pyramids" in Africa have neither exterior staircases, nor temples, nor even a summit for a temple to stand on.

The Great Pyramids at Teotihuacan, however, had all those things; exterior staircases, summits, temples on the summits, and tiers.

Working from the records of Spanish conquistadors, the historian William H. Prescott left descriptions of the temples that stood atop the Great Pyramids at Teotihuacan:

"Distinct traces of [temples] are said to be visible on the summit of the smaller pyramid, consisting of the remains of stone walls showing a building of considerable size and strength. There are no remains on the top of the pyramid of the Sun...

"The summit of this larger mound is said to have been crowned by a temple, in which was a colossal statue of its presiding deity, the Sun, made of one entire block of stone, and facing the east. Its breast was protected by a plate of burnished gold and silver, on which the first rays of the rising luminary rested. An antiquary, in the early part of the last century [1700's], speaks of having seen some fragments of the statue. It was still standing, according to report, on the invasion of the Spaniards, and was demolished by the indefatigable Bishop Zumarraga, whose hand fell more heavily than that of Time itself on the Aztec monuments.

"Around the principal pyramids are a great number of smaller ones, rarely exceeding thirty feet in height, which, according to tradition, were dedicated to the stars, and served as sepulchers for the great men of the nation. They are arranged symmetrically in avenues terminating at the sides of the great pyramids, which face the cardinal points. The plain on which they stand was called *Micoatl*, or 'Path of the Dead.' "xxxviii

After removing the error of calling the pyramids in Africa, "the Great Pyramids," it became possible to concentrate on another Wonder of the World that was at Heliopolis-Teotihuacan.

Probably during the 5th century BC, Herodotus visited the Labyrinth. He wrote:

"After the reign of the priest of Hephaestus the Egyptians were made free. But they could never live without a king, so they divided Egypt into twelve portions and set up twelve kings...Moreover they resolved to preserve the memory of their names by some joint enterprise; and having so resolved they made a labyrinth, a little way beyond the lake Moeris and near the place called the City of Crocodiles. I have myself seen it, and indeed no words can tell its wonders; were all that Greeks have builded and wrought added together the whole would be seen to be a matter of less labour and cost than was this labyrinth, albeit the temples at Ephesus and Samos are noteworthy buildings. Though the pyramids were greater than words can tell, and each one of them a match for many great monuments built by Greeks, this maze surpasses even the pyramids. It has twelve roofed courts, with doors over against each other: six face the north and six the south, in two continuous lines, all within one outer wall. There are also double sets of chambers, three thousand altogether, fifteen hundred above and the same number under ground. We ourselves viewed those that are above ground, and speak of what we have seen; of the underground chambers we were only told; the Egyptian wardens would by no means show them, these being, they said, the burial vaults of the kings who first built this labyrinth, and of the sacred crocodiles. Thus we can only speak from hearsay of the lower chambers; the upper we saw for ourselves, and they are creations greater than human. The outlets of the chambers and the mazy passages hither and thither through the courts were an unending marvel to us as we passed from court to apartment and from apartment to colonnade, from colonnades again to more chambers and then into yet more courts. Over all this is a roof, made of stone like the walls, and the walls are covered with carven figures, and every court is set round with pillars of white stone most exactly fitted together. Hard by the corner where the labyrinth ends there stands a pyramid forty fathoms high, whereon great figures are carved...Such is this labyrinth... "[xxxix]

Archaeologist Rene Millon discovered that same maze-like design built into a group of buildings at Teotihuacan. This maze of buildings at Teotihuacan had over a thousand rooms, and it sprawled out beside the "Pyramid of the Moon," exactly where Herodotus said the Labyrinth was built.

Regarding the maze of winding passages and the lack of entrances at the structure in Teotihuacan, Millon wrote:

"The apartment compounds consisted of different apartments joined by passages for circulation; they had domestic sanctuaries, and the entire compound was surrounded by an exterior wall. Apartments generally consisted of several rooms at slightly different levels, arranged around open patios. They were designed for maximum privacy; each construction was isolated from the street and the exterior walls had no windows; generally *only one entrance* led to the outside. "[xl]

Besides its strange maze design, there was another discovery about this labyrinth at Teotihuacan that baffled archaeologists and modern scholars:

"[Teotihuacan] burials are rich in information. However, with one exception…the number of adults interred in each one of the compounds is too low, relative to the area of the compound, to account for most of its inhabitants…Perhaps other adults, particularly women, were buried in other places."[xli]

According to Herodotus the ancient Egyptians had built this Labyrinth primarily as a burial place for *kings*. That explained the near-absence of female remains in the labyrinth at Teotihuacan.

The discovery of Heliopolis in Mexico could provide great relief to modern scholars who have been baffled by the disappearance of so monumental a city from the Egypt in Africa. The German Egyptologist Adolph Erman revealed the dilemma after visiting the site of the missing city. He wrote:

"About 19 miles to the north of Memphis, north-east of the bend of the river, was the ancient sacred city of On, better known to us by its Greek name, Heliopolis.

This name, 'City of the Sun,' shows us which god was revered here; the temple was one of the most splendid in the country, and according to Herodotus, the priests were considered the wisest in Egypt. A great part of the ancient Egyptian religious literature appears to have been written in this town. At the present day...one obelisk stands alone to point out the spot to visitors."[xlii]

At that site in Africa, there is no monumental road, no Labyrinth, no Great Pyramids built in a tier design with staircases and temples on their summits, and no evidence of the great lakes, dams and cities that became known as Ta-She, Wonder of the World.

Some have pointed to a stone obelisk in a field in northeast Africa and explained that is the proof that Heliopolis was there.

Heliopolis did not vanish from the planet. It simply became another secret in the *Forbidden Histories* of the Americas.

Chapter 17

"A Dark Denial"

When I offered the discovery of Heliopolis to a professor at Texas Christian University (TCU) for review, he wrote back that Herodotus was not a credible historian. I had not anticipated that response, but I knew immediately what his reply meant and I knew that no serious review could be gained from him.

It was well known that Herodotus was accorded the honor, "Father of History," because his peers respected his knowledge on historical subjects. More recently, distinguished Egyptologists, such as Adolph Erman, had often rested their knowledge about ancient Egypt on some foundation provided by Herodotus.

Still, the TCU professor and some other modern scholars preferred to distance themselves from Herodotus because of a racial secret that Herodotus let out about history. Herodotus wrote:

"...it is plain to see that the Colchians are Egyptians; and this that I say I myself noted before I heard it from others. When I began to think on this matter, I inquired of both peoples; and the Colchians remembered the Egyptians better than the Egyptians remembered the Colchians; the Egyptians said that they held the Colchians to be part of Sesostris' army. I myself guessed it to be so, partly because they are black skinned and woolly-haired; though that indeed goes for nothing, seeing that other peoples, too, are such; but my better proof was that the Colchians and Egyptians and Ethiopians are the only nations that have from the first practiced circumcision."

Herodotus had undraped for modern eyes that the ancient Egyptians were "black skinned and woolly-haired." Some modern scholars began to quote Herodotus to assert that Black Africans (as Egyptians) had built the foundation of Western civilization. Other scholars—wanting desperately to believe that Black Africans should have no part in the development of Western civilization, or any civilization—chose to discredit Herodotus.

The TCU professor's comment about Herodotus made it clear where his sensitivities resided. It did not matter that the pre-Columbian city, Teotihuacan, mirrored ancient descriptions of Heliopolis. What mattered more to the professor was that Herodotus could not be given credence, for anything. To do otherwise would open the door for black-skinned people to be Egyptians, and there were too many uncomfortable consequences standing behind that door.

Chapter 18

"A Wondrous island called Memphis"

When Dr. George Kelm was asked to review a portion of the findings, he, after reading parts of the research, gave a disheartening piece of advice. He stated that I could not re-establish the ancient cities in the Americas without removing the cities in Europe, Asia and Africa that now claim to be the cities discussed in the ancient histories.

I understood what he meant and I was undaunted by the challenge. I had found that, like Heliopolis, other important cities named in the ancient histories were standing on phantom foundations in the "Old World." Egypt's ancient Memphis was no exception.

On August 26, 1998, I saw the scholars' notes that Heliopolis was missing. That same day, I saw their notes showing that Memphis, too, had disappeared.

Notes from German Egyptologist Adolph Erman were the first to allow me to see that Memphis did not exist along the Nile. Erman had written:

"We will…confine ourselves to the description of certain important towns … The old capital of Egypt, Memphis (Mennufer), naturally stands first; it was situated a little above the modern Cairo on the west

85

bank of the river. It *has entirely disappeared*. ... The famous citadel of the town, the 'White Wall,' as well as the other buildings, *have utterly vanished,* evidently owing to the fact that the inhabitants of the neighboring Cairo used the ruins of Memphis as a convenient quarry."[xliii]

Notice the "evidently" clause in Erman's attempt to explain how a large city like Memphis could "vanish" from the planet.

The fact that no trace of a city can be found is not "evidence" that its stones, bricks, canals, pyramids, walls—and even its man-made lakes—were moved to another place. Instead, when *nothing* remains of a city that was as greatly built as Memphis, it is evidence that the city was *"evidently"* not there.

The learned Egyptologist, Brugsch, was forced, like Erman, to declare that the large and once-populous city called Memphis had entirely disappeared. He wrote, "The repeated excavations which have been undertaken in our day on the site of Memphis have given results hardly worth naming..."[xliv]

Brugsch, needing to explain how a monumental, pyramided capital city could vanish, offered the same explanation that Erman had conjured, "...the immense masses of stone used in the building of the temples have been in the course of time transported to Cairo, to supply the materials needed for the mosques, palaces, and houses of the city of the Khalifs."[xlv]

Any scholar who echoes the usual explanation for the disappearance of Memphis ("it was disassembled to build Cairo") must not be familiar with medieval Arab writings about Memphis. One Arab traveler described Memphis as still standing in its monumental splendor as late as the 13th century AD.[xlvi]

Yet, Memphis has now "disappeared" from Africa.

There was no long search to find ancient Memphis. Finding Heliopolis in Mexico had narrowed the area to be searched. Then Aztec histories and ancient Egyptian and Greek accounts about Memphis made it clear that the island where the Aztec capital had stood was also the island where Memphis had been.

Egyptian priests at Heliopolis told Herodotus about the swamp, the crocodiles and the building of Memphis. The Greek historian then wrote:

"The priests told me that Min was the first ["human"] king of Egypt, and that first he separated Memphis from the Nile by a dam. All the river had flowed close under the sandy mountains on the Libyan side, but Min made the southern bend of it which begins about an hundred furlongs above Memphis, by damming the stream; thereby he dried up the ancient course, and carried the river by a channel so that it flowed midway between the hills. And to this day the Persians keep careful guard over this bend of the river, strengthening its dam every year, that it may keep the current in; for were the Nile to burse his dykes and overflow here, all Memphis were in danger of drowning. Then, when this first king Min had made what he thus cut off to be dry land, he first founded in it that city which is now called Memphis—for even Memphis lies in the narrow part of Egypt—and outside of it he dug a lake to its north and west, from the river (the Nile itself being the eastern boundary of the place); and secondly, he built in it the great and most noteworthy temple of Hephaestus."[xlvii]

The dams and tall causeways built, or rebuilt, by Menes to create the island of Memphis were such marvels that Memphis was often referred to as *"The Wall."*

The engineering skills required to construct those great dams and other water-controlling inventions were so extraordinary, that, together with the resulting lakes, this effort was acknowledged as one of the Seven Wonders of the Ancient World.

In Egypt's ancient writings, this lake region was sometimes called simply "Ta-She." The Aztecs knew that name and called the great lake "TESHEE-KOKO" (Texcoco).

Working against a map of the Aztec lake left by historian William Prescott, and with descriptions provided by Herodotus, the island city called Memphis, and its famed lakes, bloomed into view.

Herodotus revealed, *"…[Min] separated Memphis from the Nile by a dam."*

And the Prescott map showed the causeway and dam that separated the island from the lake.

Herodotus wrote, *"All the river had flowed close under the sandy mountains on the Libyan side, but Min made the*

88

southern bend of it which begins about an hundred furlongs above Memphis, by damming the stream;"

The Prescott map showed the dam that caused the water to bend back to the south. Herodotus explained that this dam was situated "a hundred furlongs" from the city. A hundred furlongs is nearly 13 miles. The Prescott map showed that southern bend of the lake turning exactly where Herodotus said the bend was.

Herodotus wrote, *"were the Nile to burse his dykes and overflow here, all Memphis were in danger of drowning."*

The Prescott map showed that the island was situated directly in front of the Mexicalcingo-Coyoacan dam. A break in that dam would have caused an immense surge of the pent-up waters in Lake Xochimilco to rush directly over the island city.

The presence of the name "Nile" in that description did not affect the discovery. Regarding this "Nile," Herodotus wrote: "The river flows from the west and the sun's setting." The river now being called "Nile," in northeast Africa, does not flow from west to east; it flows from the south to the north.

Against every record I found of ancient Memphis, the island in the Valley of Mexico did not fail to match each nuance of the descriptions of this capital city of Lower Egypt.

Chapter 19

"A crocodile in the Lake of the Moon"

Egypt's priests had revealed to Herodotus how the flood-prone, swampy site in the Valley of Mexico had been drained; how the land was dug out to form artificial lakes; and how a mound of land was left standing to create the manmade island that became Memphis. Here was the great and secret "primeval mound" that had eluded and puzzled scholars for centuries.

Looking at Prescott's map, it was obvious that the great lakes around the island were intentionally dug out to create the likeness of a crocodile. The lake at the north end formed the head of the crocodile. The lake called Texcoco formed the body of the crocodile, while Lake Xochimilco was channeled into the likeness of a crocodile's tail.

The reason for the crocodile design of the lakes around this island was this:

"The worship of the gods, the temple services, and the cult of Apis were introduced by *Menes,* who is said to have been *devoured by a crocodile.*"[xlviii]

The builder of Memphis had been killed and eaten by a crocodile.

It was amazing to see the Aztec histories also remember this disastrous attack by a crocodile on the ruler who had built this island city in Mexico. The Aztecs gave this man the name *"Tezcatlipoca"* and they said of this king:

"The most powerful of the earthly spirits was Tezcatlipoca …. In the night sky the symbol of the god Tezcatlipoca could be seen as the group of stars we call the Great Bear. To the Aztecs, this was the single footprint of the god who had lost his other foot when he drew the earth out of the waters in the titanic struggle before mankind was created. The god tempted the Earth Monster to come to the surface of the waters and drew her on with his enormous foot. The gigantic monster snapped off his foot, but he in turn tore off her lower jaw, and she never again sank back into the waters. On her rugged back all the tribes of men were created and lived."[xlix]

It was this island—which appeared to float on the "back" of the crocodile-shaped lake—that was meant by the Aztec expression, *"On her rugged back all the tribes of men were created and lived."*

This history of Menes-Tezcatlipoca and the crocodile could explain why the district of Memphis was known as "Crocodilopolis."

The history of the Aztec's Tezcatlipoca mirrors the history of Egypt's Menes, just as the Aztec island city mirrored descriptions of Memphis.

91

The meaning of the design of the west lake, showing a woman carrying the island on her back, is explained by Egypt's sacred traditions about the Egyptian deity called Heru. Some ancient Greek writers called this deified Pharaoh, "Horus."

Before Heru was born, his mother was forced to hide on an island, to protect this hereditary prince from being murdered by another lord who wanted to rule Egypt. As a young child, Heru stayed hidden on the island and was carried on the back of the woman called Isis, or her sister called Neith. The boy survived the murder attempts, survived a bloody war with the biblical Cain, became Pharaoh, and eventually became one of the most venerated deities in all of Egypt.

The Prescott map shows the west lake to form the outlined image of a woman, with the island appearing to be held against her back by the straight lines of the causeways, which form the image of straps.

Isis and Neith were deified and received the moon as their symbol. It was for this reason that Aztecs called the female-shaped lake on the west side of Memphis-Tenochtitlan, "the Lake of the Moon."

The Aztecs wrote, "...the great city of Tenochtitlan (was) built on islands at the centre of *the Lake of the Moon.*"[1]

The ingenious designs of the crocodile-shaped great lakes, the Lake of the Moon, the manmade island, the Great Pyramids at Teotihuacan, the famed Labyrinth, and the great Road of the Gods—all these

WHEN ROCKS CRY OUT

things endured long enough to show that Memphis and Heliopolis had existed in the Americas, in Mexico.

Spain demolished the island city of Tenochtitlan and drained most of the lakes around that island. Archaeologists are now uncovering the ancient ruins at this site that was Memphis. The pyramids buried beneath today's Mexico City are coming back into view.

However, unless the world is successful in changing the bias against the pre-Columbian African presence, the ancient Egyptian artifacts being unearthed in Mexico may continue to be funneled, secretly, into the Museum of Egyptian art at Mexico, or into other Egyptian museums around the world, with no acknowledgment that the Egyptian artifacts were discovered in Mexico.

Chapter 20

"A Pharaoh's voyage maps the Americas"

While the *National Geographic* historian reviewed the Memphis and Heliopolis findings, I returned to the stones that had unlocked the secret of Egypt in the Americas.

A stone called the Piankhi Stele took hold of my senses. It was a pinkish granite stone, covered with hieroglyphs. An historian copied the story of this stele and began selling copies of it in 1867. An American Egyptologist wrote of those copies, "This work was for some reason withdrawn from sale a few days after publication, and only the few copies sold now exist."

The Piankhi Stele reveals the location of Memphis and Heliopolis in Mexico. The inscriptions also mention several other important cities along Piankhi's route to Mexico. Even the famed Troy is shown, in its Egyptian name.

The stele tells us that Pharaoh Meriamon Piankhi received word that Egypt was under attack and that major cities were being taken from Egypt's empire. Piankhi dispatched an army with instructions to perform religious rites at Thebes, and then to proceed north on a campaign to re-capture the cities.

When his army sent word that the Egyptian soldiers could not retake some of the larger cities, Piankhi led another army "north," from Thebes, on a campaign that reached from South America to the Valley of Mexico.

When historians attempted to fit the history from the Piankhi Stele into the small area of the Egypt in Africa, impossible problems developed.

Piankhi sailed from South America, going north. He reached a fortress called on the stele, "Mer-Atum." This may be the ruined fortress now called Tulum, but I am not sure of this.

After recapturing Mer-Atum, Piankhi sailed again then landed at another port. He marched inland on the Yucatan Peninsula to an ancient religious center, which appears to be the Maya city Chichen Itza. The stele calls that place, *"Ithtowe,"* which may be a reference to the word "Itza" in Chichen Itza.

The Piankhi Stele tells us:

"His majesty sailed north to Ithtowe; he found the rampart closed, and the walls filled with the valiant troops of the Northland. Then they opened the stronghold, and threw themselves upon [their] bellies [before] his majesty (saying): 'Thy father has assigned to thee his inheritance. Thine are the Two Lands, thine is what is therein, thine is all that is on earth.' His majesty entered to cause a great oblation to be offered to the gods residing in this city..."

At the point where Piankhi leaves Chichen Itza, something is written on the stele that confused the translators and historians. The stele shows that, after leaving Chichen Itza, Piankhi sailed *"west"*!

95

Historians, trying to follow the stele, believed Piankhi was traveling northward down the Nile. But how could Piankhi sail *"west"* before he reached the end of the Nile?

Unable to make sense of this western turn out of the Nile River, Breasted injected his own words into the hieroglyphic account. He changed the direction given on the stele, and wrote that Piankhi sailed "northward," but Breasted enclosed the word "northward" in parentheses to show that the Piankhi Stele did not say "northward."

Actually, Piankhi really did sail westward. He was following the coast of the Yucatan Peninsula, which took him westward, then southward toward the Valley of Mexico. That was the natural course of the sea route to reach Mexico from Chichen Itza; and Piankhi was headed to Memphis, the island city built in the lake in the Valley of Mexico.

When Piankhi reached Memphis, he faced ingenuous defenses—including an island city that was surrounded by lakes:

"When day broke, at early morning, his majesty reached Memphis. When he had landed on the north of it, he found that the water had approached to the walls, the ships mooring at [the walls of] Memphis. Then his majesty saw that it was strong, and that the wall was raised by a new rampart and battlements manned with mighty men. There was found no way of attacking it. Every man told his opinion among the army of his majesty, according to every rule of war. Every man said: 'Let us besiege [it]--; lo, its troops are numerous.' Others said: 'Let a causeway be made against it; let us elevate the ground to its walls. Let us bind together a tower; let us erect masts and make the spars into a bridge to it. We will divide it on this (plan) on every side of it, on the high ground and on the north of it, in order to elevate the ground at its walls, that we may find a way for our feet.'

"Then his majesty was enraged against it like a panther; he said: 'I swear, as Re loves me, as my father, Amon [who fashioned me], favors me, this shall befall it, according to the command of Amon .... I will take it like a flood of water.'

"Then he sent forth his fleet and his army to assault the harbor of Memphis; they brought to him every ferry-boat, every [cargo] boat, every [transport], and the ships, as many as there were, which had moored in the harbor of Memphis, with the bow-rope fastened among its houses.

"His majesty himself came to line up the ships, as many as there were. His majesty commanded his army (saying): 'Forward against it! Mount the walls! Penetrate the houses over the river. If one of you gets through upon the wall, let him not halt before it, [so that] the (hostile) troops may not repulse you. It were vile that we should close up the South, should land [in] the North and lay siege in *Balances of the Two Lands*.' "

Attempting to fit the event onto the Nile in Africa, some translators of the Piankhi Stele interpreted the water around Memphis to be a "river." The correct interpretation of those hieroglyphs should probably be *lakes*. The stele had already explained that water was all around the island city of Memphis.

Not one or two walls, but *all* of the sides of Memphis were against waters of the lakes:

"When he had landed on the north of it, he found that the water had approached to the *walls*, the ships mooring at [the walls of] Memphis."

The Piankhi Stele reveals that Memphis was an island, with causeways needed to reach it.

"Let a *causeway* be made against it; let us elevate the ground to its walls... We will divide it on this (plan) *on every side of it*, on the high ground and on the north of it, in order to elevate the ground at its walls, *that we may find a way for our feet.*"

For the benefit of those who would suggest that the passage, *"let us elevate the ground to its walls..."* means filling in a depression with dirt, Piankhi would later use "boats" to "find a way for our feet."

After capturing Memphis, the stele tells us that Piankhi left Memphis to visit the near-by city of Heliopolis, which stood across the lakes and to the east of Memphis.

Arriving in Heliopolis-Teotihuacan, Piankhi went up the great, central street of the gods. The Piankhi Stele called it *"the highway of the god."* Nearly three thousand years later, pre-Columbian traditions of Mexico continue to refer to that same street as *"the road of the Gods."*

Using the "road of the Gods" to ascend the hill to reach the Sun Pyramid, Piankhi stopped to purify himself in the waters of the city. Then the Pharaoh went to the Pyramid of the Sun to offer sacrifices. According to Breasted's interpretation of the Piankhi Stele, the Sun Pyramid was called *"the Sand-hill."*

The Pyramid of the Sun at Teotihuacan was called "Sand-hill," because its interior is composed of dirt."[li]

The Piankhi Stele then confirms that this Pyramid of the Sun had a stair-case and a temple on its summit:

"He ascended the steps to the great window, to behold Re in the *pyramidion-house.* The king himself stood alone, he broke through the bolts, opened the double doors, and beheld his father, Re, in the glorious pyramidion-house…"

According to the stele, Piankhi also sacrificed to former Egyptian kings in a sacred cavern beneath the Pyramid of the Sun. That cavern continues to exist beneath the Pyramid of the Sun at Teotihuacan.[lii]

The Piankhi Stele had confirmed the American locations of the island called Memphis and the stair-cased pyramid at Heliopolis.

The stele also helped me to see another Egyptian capital. Thebes, I believed, had been a large, walled city in the Andes Mountain of South America. The Piankhi Stele made it clear that Thebes was far to the south and across a sea from the Yucatan Peninsula. Nothing in the Piankhi Stele argued against Thebes being in South America.

I tested and retested ancient descriptions of the ruined city in South America. I had Thebes!

Then something happened that threw cold water on the whole affair.

Chapter 21

"In the eye of the storm"

The first time I noticed the words *"the West"* on ancient Egyptian stones, I thought Egyptians had visited the Americas on some infrequent sea voyages.

I knew better now.

The old stones were ready to tell anyone who would listen that those Africans had built an Egypt in the Americas before they built the monument-filled Egypt in northeast Africa. The ancient histories explained that the Africans came to the Americas and built cities from Brazil to Mexico, and possibly further north.

Those who attempted to trace Egypt's ancient history against the much smaller expanse of land along the Nile in Africa ran into geographic problems that were impossible to untangle. The distances between the places in the hieroglyphic texts and the time it took to travel between the places just did not make sense against the landscape of the modern Middle East. Those ancient histories needed an area that was as far-reaching as the distance from the Nile in northeast Africa to the Valley of Mexico in the Americas.

It was clear that there was an Egypt on the Nile, *and* an Egypt in the Americas, but early in the search, I had not discovered when or why Egypt had left the Americas to build the Egypt in the East.

That problem did not keep me from dropping to my knees and thanking God for what He had allowed me to see. I was not stupid enough to think that the findings were the fruit of my intellect. There had been too many things that had fallen into my possession in the most unusual way—things that I never knew existed.

And so, I prayed—often.

It was at the end of a prayer, during the winter of 1998, that something was told to me that froze my muscles where I could not move. Then I felt my body begin to shake as if I had fallen into the grip of pneumonia. Someone in the house came to the door of the room where I was and asked me if I was talking to them. Words about the thing that had frozen me had slipped past my lips, loud enough to be heard in another room. I hadn't heard my own words.

"Were you talking to me?" my son was asking. "Dad, are you praying?"

I closed the prayer, knowing I had to return to it again shortly.

"Uh….yeah, son, I was…..I was praying."

I *had* been praying, but Understanding took my thoughts and made me understand that the things being shown to me were not about Egypt.

The events of the Bible had happened in the lands south of where I lived. The Exodus had occurred in the Americas! Christ had been born here. During the prayer, I saw it!

How could I tell a planet full of people that someone had despised them so desperately that an explosive lie had been poured into the world's most cherished hope—its religions!

Question after question made itself felt across my thoughts. *"Who would have done such a thing? And why? Why hadn't anyone said anything about it? How could a world, filled with scholars, not see what I could see?*

"If Jerusalem and Bethlehem are in the Americas, where are they? How can I find them? Who can show me where they are?"

Even after realizing that the search was about something deeper than finding ancient Egypt, I stayed slumped over the desk. Everything that I had been shown was swirling in and out of my thoughts. I couldn't stop the pieces to put them in order. Somehow, I put myself in a bed that night, but I didn't remember how or when.

For nearly a week, I moved around in a daze. Everything had suddenly become very serious to me. How could I smile, knowing what I now knew?

When I prayed, there was no answer. It probably did not come because I already knew the answer. I was asking in my prayers if I could just tell the world about Egypt, without mentioning the other thing. I did not have to ask for an answer to that. I had been given a great thing, and then I was given a deadly thing to go with it. Not only would people hate me for bringing this, but nations would consider my death—nations like Israel, which piles up great wealth with their claims of being the Holy Land, of being the place where the Christ had lived and died.

I had seen the past. Even Israel was not in Israel. How could I say that to the world, or to anyone?

I tried. I sat down with preachers to try to tell them what I had found.

There was one preacher who lived in a town that was on the outskirts of my own city, toward the sunrise. In three attempts to speak with him about what I had seen, none was successful. Still, a preacher in my town had pointed to him as being knowledgeable enough to judge the things that had been uncovered. So I went to his church, uninvited, near the end of a Wednesday Night Service. He tried to avoid the discussion, but somehow we wound up at a table, with me showing him what had been found.

When it was over, the preacher expelled the air that had built up inside of him. Then he spoke.

"There is no doubt that Egypt was in the Americas. I can see that clearly with what you have shown. But I cannot, I will not, concede that the things of the Old Testament happened in the Americas. I don't care what you show me, I will not believe that. I can't believe that."

I was not shocked by his words, but I was disheartened. He had given a similar answer on the telephone without seeing anything I had. He had said that he "wouldn't have the heart to believe it, even if it were true."

I gathered together the maps and the papers, and stuffed them into the leather bag with the books. Nothing in the books would have any worth this night.

During the drive back home, I thought about the Old Testament's Jonah. So many preachers had laughed in their sermons about this man. Jonah was a preacher who was afraid to take a hard message to a tough group of people. When he tried to sail away from the problem, a whale swallowed Jonah. Preachers laughed at that, saying Jonah should have known that you can not run from God.

Now Jonah's "fish" was on the preachers' table, and they did not recognize the whale.

I had to go where even Jonah would not go, and I had no preacher to walk with me. Now when I prayed, I asked God to guide my ink and to give me strength.

I had no idea how appropriate the prayer for strength would come to be. Every time I made an effort to get the findings announced or printed, ruin would suddenly visit something around me. An arrogant man with no love for understanding would say that my ruin was the sign of a sin. A man of more wisdom would recall the man in the biblical narrative called *Job*. I could never forget the Old Testament's *Job*.

In the midst of all my ruin, one whisper kept visiting me, "Be peaceful. All things are in my hand."

Chapter 22

"Map of the Pharaoh in New Orleans"

In the days that followed my comprehension that the discoveries were about the Christ, my understanding went blank. For several weeks, I could not write anything that seemed to make sense. Each piece of my understanding about the ancient Americas had emerged from some earlier piece of comprehension. Suddenly, the pieces had begun to flit through my thoughts in chaos. I tried, but I could not think the pieces back into sensible order again. My comprehension of the ancient histories was vanishing.

When the writing failed to return to my fingers, I began reading what I had written earlier—again and again—attempting to re-kindle the understanding, but the comprehension stayed hidden. I could get no grasp on the route of the Exodus in the Americas. No more cities came to me like Memphis and Heliopolis had.

I began concentrating on a place that was named on a stone concerning Ramses. The place called Kadesh continued to turn up in the ancient writings. Some mapmakers and historians argued that Kadesh was north of the place now being called Jerusalem. Others argued that ancient Kadesh was located near the Red Sea, at the *southern* end of the Sinai Peninsula.

Kadesh had become a modern *Riddle of the Sphinx*. Scholars, historians and writers simply could not agree on the location of Kadesh. Some biblical scholars were so discomfited by the failure of Kadesh to fit into the Middle East landscape that they began to argue that there must have been many places called Kadesh.

For some reason, my interest kept running toward ancient accounts of an Egyptian battle with the people called Kheta, at Kadesh. I would read the accounts about the Kheta, see nothing there and then close the account. The next day, I could not keep myself from repeating that same routine. The Kheta became an obsession. I could not determine the reason for the obsession.

Biblical scholars excluded, most historians placed the Kheta people and their city, Kadesh, near a major river, and since no such river was in the southern part of the Sinai Peninsula, Kadesh was argued to be in the north, near the river now being called Orontes.

Ignoring the ancient histories that place Kadesh on a river, biblical scholars continued to stress that the Old Testament makes it clear that Kadesh was located at the southern end of the Sinai Peninsula. Those scholars argued that the biblical narratives place the Hebrews in Kadesh immediately after they left the land of Egypt. Here are the Old Testament accounts they pointed to:

"...Israel came up from Egypt, and walked through the wilderness unto the Red sea, and came to Kadesh" (Judg: 11:16)

WHEN ROCKS CRY OUT

"Then came the children of Israel, even the whole congregation, into the desert of Zin in the first month: and the people abode in Kadesh; and Miriam died there, and was buried there." (Num 20:1)

I knew without a doubt that Kadesh was going to be found somewhere in the Americas. After several weeks, I still had not found Kadesh and I became anxious because the secrets, and the *feelings*, had deserted me.

Each time that I felt I had discovered the location of Kadesh, the place would fail the test of some historical account.

I did not know why I could not let go of Kadesh. No matter how I reasoned with myself, I could not get the thought of Kadesh out of my mind.

My wife noticed that my mental travels into the ancient past were stretching further and further into the night. I heard her approach me as I sat in the darkness of the room, washed by the light of the computer monitor.

"Hey, the kids and I are thinking about going down to New Orleans this weekend. You want to come?"

She knew me too well. I never turn down a trip to New Orleans. Just hearing the sound of the name seems to turn on some coffee-like aroma in my mind. I could smell a New Orleans morning from 600 miles away.

"Don't you want a break? I already have the room reserved," she urged.

My daydreaming of New Orleans had kept me from answering her first query.

"Yeah, that's probably what I need, some New Orleans."

Then I did what I had not been able to do for months. I closed the pages of every book that lay scattered and stacked around the room—and turned the lights out on them.

To be honest, the only repose from the search was the drive down to New Orleans. Even during the drive through the tight downtown traffic on the way to the hotel, I found myself peering down side streets, looking for a used-book store. I spotted an old rare-books store a block or so before we reached the hotel. That would be the first stop after we were settled into the room.

An hour later, I was pulling open the heavy faded French door of the store. Something didn't feel right about the place. Unlike the bookstores in my neighborhood back home, there were no people in this one, except for me and the clerk. After peeling through several books on ancient Egypt and ancient America, I headed back into the smells and sounds of New Orleans.

Two blocks from the book store, I noticed I had somehow missed turning onto the familiar street that led to the marketplace near the Mississippi River. It really didn't matter, you just walk when you're in New Orleans—every block and every weather-worn cranny can hold something interesting.

I don't know what made me stop and look back across the street, maybe simple curiosity, but a small sign slightly swinging above one of the many tall French doors pulled at my attention.

"The Centuries Antique Prints and Maps."

This was New Orleans. You never knew what you'd find in this timeless city. The market along the river would have to wait

I pushed against the heavy, glass-centered door and a few small bells signaled my entry. Around the perimeter of the room were mat-framed maps, organized on their edges in wooden bins. An old map of Brazil drew me close to the wall to get a better view of the hanging illustration. A date from the 1800's was penciled onto the mat frame. Something about the map suddenly shooed the butterflies in my stomach.

I pronounced the names on the map for my own hearing. I was looking for faintly concealed places that the hieroglyphs had mentioned. Then, I saw "Bahia...Para...Piauhi....Piauhi? PIANKHI?!"

I pulled down the map to get a closer look.

"MARANHAM PIAUHI!!!" The sound had come out of my mouth louder than I had intended. The woman clerk and the two other people in the small room jerked their eyes toward the sound that had tenored across my lips.

PIAUHI. I knew this name. This was the Pharaoh who ruled Egypt before Taharque. It was this "Piauhi" whose re-conquest of the Americas was preserved on the Piankhi Stele—the same Piankhi who landed at Memphis in the Valley of Mexico and climbed the stairs of the pyramid at Heliopolis-Teotihuacan. The ancient Egyptian records called him *"Meriamon-Piankhi."*

Here was the name of that Pharaoh spread across a large area in eastern Brazil—in the Americas!

I turned to speak to the woman who appeared to be the owner of the store. She was on the phone and had another woman waiting to speak with her.

I couldn't just stand there, not with the way my pulse was drumming. I walked back to the bins and flipped through another stack of the matted maps, but I saw no more maps of South America.

Another customer had come in. I moved next to the smiling customer who had sat down beside the store keeper. She was getting too comfortable for a short question.

"Excuse me," I asked, out of turn, "Do you know if you have any more maps of Brazil, from this period?"

I had to know if this one map was some unorthodox fantasy design.

"Yes, we have several maps from that era and earlier, I believe. Look in that bin to your right, in the center."

The next South American map I found had less detail than the one I was holding. Two maps deeper into the bin, my mouth fell apart. The map showed the name "Egypt" on the area right below Piauhi's name! It was written "Seregipe Del Rey." My comprehension quickly pushed the prefix *"Ser"* away from *"egipe."* When I looked again, at the first map, *Seregipe* was printed on it, too!

I closed my eyes and whispered a prayer.

My wife had reasoned that the trip would allow me to rest from the research, yet here I stood chest-high in maps showing Egypt in the Americas. Her decision to visit New Orleans could be remembered by history as one of the most important reasons why this book exists.

The three maps, together, would cost nearly a thousand dollars. The 200-year-old map with the Pharaoh's name on it was priced $700. I asked the woman if they sold reproductions of the maps. She wanted to know why the maps were having such an effect on me. After a few minutes of explaining the project, she was on the phone attempting to reach the owner, Frank Mapes. The tide was beginning to turn. I had finally found somebody who understood what I was saying.

Then the tide went back out. Mapes was not answering the phone at his home. The woman, in her most apologetic voice, said that she would continue trying to reach Mapes.

What if someone bought the map while I was gone? How would I prove that I had seen the old, rare maps that showed a land called Egypt, in South America? After what seemed like hours, I checked my watch. The store would be closing in 10 minutes. It appeared that Mapes was not going to be reached today. At a minute till closing, I thanked the clerk and asked her what time I could check with her on the next day for an answer on the maps?

"Try about 10."

I left the store and waded into the river of people that flowed like a tide on the street toward the marketplace. I realized I had no more interest for the market. Not now. I turned away from the market and made my way to the hotel.

There was a phone message waiting for me. The owner of the map store had called and asked me to phone him at his home. I wouldn't have to be anxious all night wondering whether I would be able to get the maps.

When I spoke with Frank Mapes, I was surprised that he was so interested in the findings. It was a welcomed surprise. I needed someone to share the discoveries with. The disclosures to Mapes were not greeted by the usual blatant skepticism that echoed from the all-knowing scholars at the universities. Mapes wanted to know more about each explanation that I offered.

By the end of the conversation, Mapes had assured me that I would be able to get copies of the maps.

Chapter 23

"Chasing the elusive Jordan"

It is amazing what you can see, once your eyes are opened.

I pulled one of the antique New Orleans maps upon the bed, saw a river called Mamore running through Bolivia, in South America, and knew I was looking at Hebron, where Abraham had lived, and where David had gone to.

The Mamore River. Here was the Bible's *"Mamre River."* It was the one-letter rule, again. One letter would be missing, added, or changed. Seregipe became Sergipe. "Meci-co" Became Mexico. Heru became Jeru. Egypt had named the lands "Tameri." Now the continents were called "Ameri-ca," with a "c" replacing the "t": The one-letter-rule. But I could *"see"* now.

I reached across the bed and pulled the other New Orleans map to me. My eyes moved across the antique map. Through the middle of the map flowed the Amazon River. In some places the maps showed the name of the water to be "Maranon River." The one-letter-rule. Here was the river that the Old Testament called *"Arnon."*

Maranon. Arnon. They had taken out one letter, the "r," and added the old familiar term *Mare,* a word that means large body of water. The Atlantic Sea, and sometimes the Caribbean Sea, were called on early maps, "*Mare* Del Nord" (*Sea* of the North), while the Pacific Ocean was called "*Mare* Del Sud" (*Sea* of the South).

The Maranon River, the Amazon, is so wide in places that it appears to be a sea. The Bible explained that the name "Arnon" meant "murmur," and the Scriptures called the Arnon, "the sea of murmuring."

Maybe that was why maps also gave the name "Maranon" to the Amazon River. It was a name that meant, literally, "Sea of Murmuring."

When the Exodus left Kadesh and Mount Sinai, near the Caribbean coast of South America, Moses led them through the dense forest of South America, probably following openings that rivers had cut through this wilderness. The biblical writings made it clear that the Hebrews followed the Amazon River.

Here was the biblical river "Arnon," tumbling out its waters into the Atlantic Ocean, which for some reason the Bible was calling "Jordan."

"Jordan," of the Old Testament writings, was the Atlantic Ocean!

Something was happening. My hair was standing on the back of my neck. A flush of cold raced across my back, then across my left arm. The coolness settled at the top of my head.

I closed the Bible. I stood up and walked away from the room and kept walking until I was out of the house and wrapped tightly in the blackness of night. I bent my head toward the stars.

"The Jordan River of the Bible is the Atlantic Ocean?"

114

My son had pointed out the Orion constellation the night before and now the three stars at Orion's waist helped me see the whole man again.

"You've known all of this the whole time, haven't you?"

The stars, dazzling on this dark, cloudless night, seemed to twinkle an answer.

"Of course they knew. They were there," I thought. *"Hadn't Egypt named the stars? With names from its own history?"*

I had read the whispers from the ancient African scribes. They had said they were writing the history of Egypt in the sky by naming the stars with names of people who had made the history happen. When you knew the history of those names, you knew the history of the founding of Egypt. The old scribes had written that if some nation got strong enough to wipe away Egypt's history on earth, they would not be able to reach the history that Egypt had written on the stars.

I pulled my gaze down from the sky and sank it inside my thoughts. *"Why did they call the Atlantic, 'the Jordan'?"*

Wheeling and walking quickly into the house, I grabbed the car keys and drove to the seminary.

At the library counter, I asked the African student where I could see what the ancient Hebrew words for "Jordan River" looked like. He knew just the book.

"What you need is the *Old Testament Interlinear Bible*. It will have the Hebrew text on one side and the English translation will be next to it."

That sounded too easy. After reaching the second level of the library, I found that it would take more effort that what the librarian's instructions suggested. There were numerous interlinear editions of the biblical narratives. There was a book for *Genesis,* one for *Samuel,* another one for *Deuteronomy,* and several others.

"Which one?" I whispered.

I ran my fingers across the hard spines of the books to my left. I was looking for the interlinear edition of *Exodus.* I was looking for an account of the Exodus. I assumed I would find the word "Jordan" there.

Finding no *Exodus* edition, my hands started across the edition called *Joshua.* I worked the book from its tight fit between the other interlinear volumes. I pulled out the *Genesis Interlinear* book and two other interlinear volumes, thinking one of them would show the ancient Hebrew words for the Jordan River.

Inside a small study cubicle, I opened the *Joshua Interlinear* edition somewhere near the middle of the book and began searching for the word, Jordan.

I found a Hebrew passage with the word "Jordan" written below the Hebrew symbols. When I saw the Hebrew symbols, I realized that the symbols would mean nothing to me if I didn't understand which symbol represented which English letter, or sound.

I had moved too fast.

Returning the books to a reshelving cart, I kept the *Joshua Interlinear* book for one last look.

I turned to the final chapter of *Joshua* to see how the writer concluded the story.

And there it was!

Here is what I saw in that 24th and final chapter of *Joshua:*

"Then Joshua gathered all the tribes of Israel at Shechem. He summoned the elders, leaders, judges and officials of Israel, and they presented themselves before God.

"Joshua said to all the people, 'this is what the Lord, the God of Israel, says: 'Long ago your forefathers, including Terah the father of Abraham and Nahor, lived beyond the River and worshipped other gods. But I took your father Abraham from the land beyond the River and led him throughout Canaan and gave him many descendants.'"

The first thing that was obvious was that the passage did not say that Abraham had come across *"the Jordan."* Instead, Abraham had been brought to "the land *beyond the River…"*

I strained to see the Hebrew symbols that were printed above the English words, "the River." I turned to the earlier interlinear passage I had read, where the word "Jordan" was printed. The Hebrew symbols for "Jordan" were not the same as the symbols for "the River." I glanced at the clock on the wall. There were seven minutes before the library would close.

It didn't matter. This was not going to work. There had to be a better way to see if the Hebrew narratives showed a sea instead of a river for "the Jordan."

I already had the answer. It was in my hand.

Chapter 24

"Of torrents, and floods, and rivers"

The Hebrews' flight from—and conquest of—Egypt stretched through several biblical 'books.' When I had refreshed my understanding of those biblical narratives, I turned my attention back to the words, "Jordan River."

The librarian from the seminary had given me the names of professors he thought could help me with the Hebrew symbols. The next day, I began calling.

The first two professors on the list were out of their office. A graduate student who worked for one of the scholars seemed eager to help.

"Well, I have this passage from the *Interlinear Bible*," I told her, "and I need to know what English words the Hebraic symbols stand for."

I was being cautious. I didn't want to frighten her away by telling her the Exodus had occurred in the Americas. I had learned the hard way that new ideas seemed to threaten some scholars. I was beginning to understand why.

The woman asked for the exact passage where I had found the words. I gave her the words "the River" from *Joshua*, 24th chapter, second verse. Then I gave her *Joshua*, 13th chapter, 28th verse, for the word "Jordan."

She left the phone for a few minutes then returned and told me that she would call me back with the answers.

An hour later, she informed me that the Hebraic symbols that were translated into the English words "the River" were pronounced and spelled, "hanahar."

"Nahar is the word, *river*. The prefix 'ha' means 'the'," she explained.

"As for the other word, 'Jordan,' the English translation is correct. The word in Hebrew is 'Yarden.' And it is the name of the Jordan River," she offered.

I believed that Joshua meant Abraham had crossed some part of the Atlantic Ocean to reach South America. While the receptionist was tracking down the Hebraic spellings, I had searched my notes again. There were two more questions that could clear up whether the water called Jordan was an ocean, and not a stream.

"I understand that you are saying the Hebraic word for *Jordan* and the Hebraic word for *river* do not have the same Hebraic spelling. What about the word, *flood?*" I asked.

"Where are you getting the word from?"

"Let's try *Joshua* again, 24th chapter, third verse. It says that Abraham was taken from the other side of 'the flood.' Do the Hebrew symbols for this word 'flood' translate into the same English letters as the word, 'river' or 'Jordan'?"

I poised the question suspecting that the answer would force out that the word "flood" would be the same as the word "river," when spelled with English letters. It would force the understanding that the word for river, "nahar" meant several kinds of water, including stream, brook, and sea.

"I knew that you were headed to that verse," the receptionist said. "I don't know what Bible you are using, but the ancient Hebrew account does not use the word, *flood*, in that passage, it uses the word, *river*, instead. Some Bibles have used the word *flood* there, but that is not what was originally written."

My eyes took hold of a verse that I had overlooked. This verse would not allow its meaning about water to be side-stepped by an unsure answer. I asked the receptionist to permit me one more passage.

I heard her expel air. I had become a nuisance.

"In the passage from *Job*, 20th chapter, 17th verse, it says, 'He shall not see the rivers, the floods, the brooks of honey and butter.' Could you tell me what letters are translated from the Hebrew symbols for rivers, floods, and brooks? All three are right together in that verse. Are the words the same for all of them?"

"Well the original passage that I'm reading didn't say 'floods,' it says, 'the rivers, the flowing of the torrents, and the brooks,'" she answered while continuing to read her text.

She excused herself from the phone for a few minutes then returned with her response.

"I am not familiar with the terms, 'flowing of the torrent.' I'm checking my *Brown Driver Bridge* and it would take me too long to look at all the words that begin with the symbols of these terms. I'm sorry. I don't know how to help you with this one."

It seemed an honest reply, but the passage had too many implications to ignore.

I telephoned the professor at the seminary who the librarian told me was "highly respected" for his knowledge of Old Testament history.

True to his doctorate nature, however, he answered my question about the three words with a question—or rather, with two questions.

"Why do you want to know? What are you trying to do with this?" he queried.

I tried to be as honest as I could without scaring him away. I told him that the words seemed to be interchanged in different places in the Bible and I wanted to know if the same Hebraic symbols were being used for several different words. It was a truthful reply.

He read through my veiled explanation and told me that what I was asking would "add nothing to the reality of what had been written."

Maybe he thought that I was attempting to build the frequent argument that there seemed to be contradictions in the Bible. To the contrary, I knew that what was written in the Bible was very exact and not contradictory, if you knew what was really written there.

He gave an answer anyway.

"The word *nahar* is actually written twice in that passage. The passage does not say, 'He shall not see the rivers, the floods, the brooks of honey and butter.' It says, 'He shall not see the rivers and the flowing torrents of honey and butter.'"

"So, the word *nahar* is used twice, once to say river, and again to say torrents? Nahar can mean something like much water?"

"Yes. The word, nahar, was used to mean several kinds of water, including river, streams, and other kinds of flowing water."

There was one last question begging for a response.

"Professor, I was told that the word for the Jordan River was 'Yarden.' Is there a history to what that word means?"

"Jordan River is Yarden nahar. The word for Jordan, 'Yarden,' comes from a root word, Y-D-N, that means, 'to descend, or descending. Going down.' It means that it descends to the Dead Sea."

"But, professor, I read an account where the Hebrews had to prepare for three days before attempting to cross the Jordan. The Jordan is only a stream. At most, it is still a very passable river. You wouldn't have to make an entire nation work for three days to cross a stream would you?"

"You have to realize that in those days it was no easy matter to cross a river. And when the Jordan was in flood. . . that could be dangerous."

I thanked the professor and did not attempt to undo his explanation, which I knew was not correct.

Jordan meant 'going down,' and 'descending.' This phrase was pulling something from my memory. Then I remembered. Some of the hieroglyphic narratives from Egypt used the terms "going down" and "descending" when Pharaohs traveled to "The West," to the "Two Lands."

I thought, initially, that when the Egyptians wrote that they "descended," they meant they had taken a sea route sailing southward along the eastern side of Africa. That seemed reasonable if they were on a route to reach South America from sea ports on the northeast side of Africa.

In the case of the Hebrews, however, the flood of water that served as the highway of "descent" to South America was the Atlantic Ocean. They called that highway of descent, "the Jordan," whose Hebrew name, Yarden, had come from the root word "YDN," which meant "to descend," or "to go down."

Later, I understood that "the Jordan" was really the name given to the Equatorial Current, that strong river-like current that runs from West Africa, cuts across the Atlantic, powers along the South American shore, past Central America and on to Mexico.

The "Jordan" is that same current the Mali sailor described when he told the Mali ruler, Abubakari, "… we met with what seemed to be a river with a strong current flowing in the open sea …"[liii]

Some pre-Columbian 'maps' show "*up*" to be toward the sunrise. Using those drawings of the world, a current in the Atlantic that rushes from West Africa to Central America would be water that descends, or that goes downward, from Africa to the Americas. The Equatorial Current, then, would certainly be a "nahar Jordan" or "water of descent."

Chapter 25

"Autobiography of Moses remembers 'Peten'"

After the secret of the Jordan was breached, an ancient Egyptian record appeared and gave the history of Moses. More than a history, the hieroglyphic record claimed to be a copy of an autobiography written by Moses. That record of Moses' life was found on several papyrus fragments and a piece of limestone.

There were some things in that record that could serve immediately. The autobiography implied that, after accidentally striking to death the Egyptian Pharaoh, Moses fled from Thebes, hurrying northward. The Bible had already told about that northward flight. But the Egyptian narrative named the place where Moses settled, "Peten"!

To anyone familiar with the names of Maya places on the Yucatan Peninsula, the mention of *Peten* in an ancient Egyptian record is a stunning discovery.

Peten is a large important region at the southern end of the Yucatan Peninsula. Biblical accounts call this place, "Pithom."

Here is the passage in the Egyptian narrative that reveals the name *Peten* as the place where Moses settled:

I ferried over, in a vessel without a rudder,
[By means of] a wind of the west.
I passed by on the east of the quarry,
Past the highland goddess, mistress of the Red
Mountain.
As I gave the way to my feet, [going *'northward'*],"
"I went on at time of evening,
As the earth brightened, I arrived at **Peten.**
When I had reached the lake of Kemwer,
I fell down for thirst...." [liv]

According to that same Egyptian record of Moses, it
was from Peten that Moses launched his great war,
which the Bible calls an exodus.

The campaign led by Moses was certainly an exodus
from Middle Egypt, but Moses had plans that went
much farther than just leaving Egypt. At the time of the
annual Egyptian Passover celebration, when Egypt was
in the throes of the national festivities that celebrated the
passage of the sun over the equator, Moses walked out
of Peten with a massive army of more than 600,000 men.
More than an exodus, Moses had planned a military
invasion of Egypt!

Chapter 26

"A mountain called Sinai, in a land called Cuyenna"

After leaving the Yucatan Peninsula's *Peten* (biblical 'Pithom'), Scriptures land the fleeing Hebrews in a place called *Kadesh*. Ancient Egyptian texts show a major river in Kadesh, and those hieroglyphics give the river's name.

Since there is no such named river on the immediate route going northward out of the Egypt in Africa, historians argued heatedly about where the Exodus had gone. Most early Egyptologists argued that the symbols in the hieroglyphic texts name the river "Y-R-S-T." Those scholars believed that the river must be the Orontes, a river that flows far north of 'that' Israel. Other scholars argued that it was ridiculous to consider the Orontes as being along the route of the Exodus.

Breasted argued that the hieroglyphics give the river's name as "Y-R-N-T." He said the name of the river was probably "Arinath."

I didn't become entangled in the confusion that engulfed these scholars. I knew the Exodus had reached South America, not the place now being called Syria.

The Orinoco River, in South America, appeared to be the river alluded to by the ancient writings.

WHEN ROCKS CRY OUT

I had the river, but I didn't have the biblical place called Kadesh.

What I *did* have was another river, the "Arnon River," which is named in the biblical narrative called *Numbers*.

According to Scriptures, after the Exodus passed Kadesh, the Hebrews followed the Arnon River.

I knew the Arnon River of the biblical inscriptions was the Amazon River.

The Arnon River (the Amazon) runs across nearly the entire width of South America, but the detailed New Orleans map showed only an eastern portion of South America. More than half the Arnon's length was missing. The route of the Exodus from Kadesh to the Amazon River could not be followed on this map.

I read the biblical accounts and then tried to comprehend places along the Amazon that were named in Scriptures.

No understanding came. I drifted back and forth on the Arnon-Amazon River, searching for the names. Every day I walked to the computer to write the next thought but nothing came. A week passed and I was still seining through biblical narratives and the autobiography of Moses, searching for understanding.

After nearly two weeks had passed, I began to worry. I could perceive no more names that Scriptures placed along the Exodus. At some point, I fenced my face within the gates of my hands and melted into the darkness. And I waited.

I heard someone ask whether I was all right, but I could not answer—not yet. For nearly an hour, I listened to the darkness.

When I raised my head, and after my eyes were able to focus on the map in front of me, I had the answer to the riddle of Kadesh.

I looked at Venezuela. Here was the land named for Isaac's son, "Esau." The old word "ben" was used to mean "son of." Some maps showed Venezuela as "Benezut." That name could mean, the land (ta) of the son (ben), Esau (ezu). 'BENEZUT.'

Some Scriptures call Venezuela, "Shur," and "Seir."

I saw the island where the famed city, "Tyre," had been. The island was still connected to the Venezuela mainland by the causeway that Alexander the Great had built to capture Tyre.

I opened the large atlas to a map of the Americas and aligned the antique New Orleans map with the page in the atlas. Then I called for my youngest son. I wanted him to see it when I saw it for the first time.

His half-trot stride bounced against the hollow-sounding upper floor until he reached the door of the room.

"What 'cha got?" he queried when he reached the back of my chair.

I pulled him toward the two maps and pointed out the starting point of the Hebrew journey, at the place called Peten. Dragging my finger across the sea that washed the eastern shores of Central America, I paused my fingertip on the northern coast of South America, at Venezuela. I would find Kadesh there—and there it was.

Some maps now call that place "Cojedes" (not to be pronounced *Ko-HA-des*, but *Kohe-DES*). Here was the biblical "Kadesh."

Near the South America region called Cojedes was the river called Orinoco.

To the east of Cojedes was a country of broad mountains. If the biblical accounts were correct, here would be found the mountain called Sinai.

A river pouring out of these South American mountains gave the first clue to Sinai. On the New Orleans map, the river is named "Cuyuni." The "Cuy" part of the name should be pronounced similar to the word 'buy,' with the 'C' in Cuy rendering its 'S' sound.

This river is the "CUY' u ni," pronounced "SUY' u ni"! That explained why the name "Sinai" is pronounced so strangely. Someone had changed the spelling of the name, but the sacred pronunciation of the name was not allowed to be changed.

The Cuyuni River flows through the country called Guyana. Most would pronounce Guyana as "Gi YAN' a." But dictionaries show there is another pronunciation: "GI' ya NA'."

The one-letter-rule had been applied again. In the name "Guyana," the letter 'G' had taken the place of the 'C' in the ancient name.

Later I saw antique maps that showed the land called Guyana to be "Cuyenna"![iv] Remembering to pronounce the "Cuy" like *buy* produced the pronunciation of Sinai, again. The older name, "Cuyenna," had been corrupted to become "Guyana."

Frank Mapes' rare maps had uncovered the elusive and extraordinary biblical region and mountain called *Sinai*.

Chapter 27

"Through serpents and a Wilderness"

West of Mount Sinai, emotional outbursts raked the air of Venezuela with high pitched African curses. The people of the Exodus complained that the Egyptians in Bolivia would kill them if they tried to take Egypt's cities in that country of famed grapes. And the Hebrews had grown frustrated with the hardships of the Exodus.

Moses returned the curses upon the people's anger, arrogance, and cowardice. Then, in resignation, he revised his ambitions and decided to lead the Hebrews to the cities of the Moabites, in eastern Brazil. Moses' father-in-law, the man who had taken in Moses when Moses fled to Peten, was a Moabite.

With his Hebrew army cowering from the idea of fighting Egypt for grape-rich Bolivia, Moses sent messengers to rulers in Guyana to request permission to pass through Guyana (Edom):

"Let us pass, I pray thee, through thy country. We will not pass through the fields, or through the vineyards, neither will we drink the water of the wells. We will go by the king's way. We will not turn to the right hand nor to the left, until we have passed thy borders.

"And Edom said unto him, Thou shalt not pass by me, lest I come out against thee with the sword.

"And the children of Israel said unto him, We will go by the high way: and if I and my cattle drink of thy water, then I will pay for it: I will only, without doing anything else, go through on my feet.

"And he said, Thou shalt not go through. And Edom came out against him with much people and with a strong hand.

"Thus Edom refused to give Israel passage through his border: wherefore Israel turned away from him." (Num 20:17-21)

The rulers in Venezuela (Seir) had granted passage to the Hebrews. Guyana refused to allow passage through that country. For this refusal, Guyana would pay dearly when the Hebrew king, Saul, gained the throne.

Guyana was called "Edom" because of something that happened to "Adam" in that country, not because "Edom" meant "red," as some reasoned.

From Kadesh, the Exodus turned and went southward into the snake infested jungles of South America. The Old Testament moves the Exodus through this wildness—or as the biblical narratives call it, *"the Wilderness."*

"And they journeyed from mount Hor by the way of the Red sea, to go around the land of Edom: and the soul of the people was much discouraged because of the way.

"And the people spake against God, and against Moses, Wherefore have ye brought us up out of Egypt to die in the wilderness? For there is no bread, neither is there any water; and our soul loatheth this light bread.

"And the LORD sent fiery serpents among the people, and they bit the people; and much people of Israel died."

Starting at the Caribbean shore of South America, I pressed my young son close to the old map and put him into the search that I anticipated would come to be historic. I urged his finger southward through Venezuela. I paused his finger when it reached a river on the map named "Cin-aruco."

The name of this river seemed to mark the biblical place called "wilderness of Cin."

At the Cinaruco River, I pressed his finger against the map and traced southward through the jungles of Brazil, until we reached the twisting line of the Amazon River (the Old Testament's "Arnon River").

The biblical narrative showed, ". . . the children of Israel set forward, and pitched in Oboth." (Num 21:4)

His small finger followed the line of the Amazon River eastward to a place that the map called "Abydos."

He looked up at me. I shrugged and nodded that it appeared to be similar to the name in the Scriptures.

I began reading again. "And they journeyed from Oboth, and pitched at Ije-abarim, in the wilderness which is before Moab, toward the sunrising."

He correctly understood "toward the sunrising" to mean toward the east. He moved his finger along the Amazon River, to the right, until it reached a large island that the map showed as "Ijoannes." The map situated this island at the place where the Amazon River emptied its waters into the Atlantic Ocean.

Following the Amazon River on the New Orleans map, his small finger had traced through places with names that seemed similar to places named in the biblical narratives. But then we came to this verse:

". . . they pitched in the valley of Zared. From thence they removed, and pitched on the other side of Arnon, which is in the wilderness that cometh out of the coasts of the Amorites: for Arnon is the border of Moab, between Moab and the Amorites.... (Num 21: 13-15)

That passage revealed that the Moabites lived on one side of the Amazon River and the Amorites lived on the other side of that river.

I did not know which side of the Amazon River the people of the Exodus had reached, because I did not know which side of the Amazon River was called Moab.

Printed on the old New Orleans map were dozens of tiny lines denoting rivers, with their names, but the letters were so small I could not read the names. The river that the Bible had called "Zered" could be among those fine lines, but I could not perceive Zared on the map, so the search ended.

Later that evening, a verse in *Joshua* helped unravel which side of the Amazon River was Moab and which was the land of the Amorites. At the beginning of the 12th chapter of *Joshua*, a river called "Jabbok" is named, and that river is described as being on the Amorite side of the Arnon (Amazon) River.

Again, it was the New Orleans map that allowed the "Jabbok" River to be seen On the old map, a mountain on the north side of the Amazon River is labeled with the name "Olympus." I knew that Olympus was associated with the deified man whom the Greeks called

133

Zeus. This "Zeus," the ancient writings explained, was really another name for Egypt's deified ruler, Ammon. It was this Ammon who was meant when Christ said "ye cannot serve God and mammon." Here, again, was the one-letter rule: they had put an "m" on Ammon's name, making it "mammon."

The biblical narratives clarified that "the children of Ammon" lived near the River Jabbok. The New Orleans map showed a mountain called "Olympus" on the north side of the Amazon. Here, the map also showed a river called "Oyapok." The map's Oyapok River appeared to be the Bible's Jabbok River.

I was not concerned that the map's name for the river was spelled with the letter *y* instead a *j*. The Jordan River was called the Yardan River with the letter 'Y' being exchanged with the letter 'J' in that name, too.

With the Jabbok River in hand, the search for the trail of the Exodus started again.

When his finger found the Jabbok River, my young son exclaimed in disbelief, "They're right here, across the Amazon River. Man, I can't believe this."

The Hebrews had journeyed from Egypt's cities in the Peten, on the Yucatan Peninsula, to the Atlantic coast of South America!

Just as amazing, Biblical narratives had remembered the names of American places along that route—for nearly 4,000 years!

Chapter 28

"At the mouth of the Amazon"

Scriptures informed that the Hebrews had settled on the opposite side of the Amazon River from the Jabbok River. The Jabbok River was on the north side of the Amazon. So, from Kadesh, Moses had led the Hebrews into cities of the Moabites on the south side of the Amazon River, near the Atlantic Ocean.

The Hebrews lived in this Moabite land for more than 30 years. Almost two thousand years later, a little boy, called both "Joshua" and "Jesus," would run and play in this same land, in a fishing village called Nazareth, which was perched on the bank on a Brazillian river that ran to the Atlantic Sea.

But now it was time for the Hebrews to move again. From south of the Amazon River, they moved northward, through a city that the Bible calls "Ar." The New Orleans map lengthens the name to "Arcos."

Continuing northward, the Hebrews crossed the Amazon-Arnon River and entered into the land of the Amorites. The narrative *Deuteronomy* reveals how an "exodus" became a military invasion of Egypt:

"Now rise up, said I, and get you over the brook Zered. And we went over the brook Zered. And the space in which we came from Kadesh-barnea, until we were come over the brook Zered, was thirty and eight years; until all the generation of the men of war were wasted out from among the host....

"So it came to pass, when all the men of war were consumed and dead from among the people, that the LORD spake unto me, saying, Thou art to pass over through *Ar, the coast of Moab*, this day: And when thou comest nigh over against the children of Ammon, distress them not, nor meddle with them: for I will not give thee of the land of the children of Ammon any possession; because I have given it unto the children of Lot for a possession.

"Rise ye up, take your journey, and pass over the river Arnon: behold, I have given into thine hand Sihon the Amorite, king of Heshbon, and his land: begin to possess it, and contend with him in battle. This day will I begin to put the dread of thee and the fear of thee upon the nations that are under the whole heaven, who shall hear report of thee, and shall tremble, and be in anguish because of thee. And I sent messengers out of the wilderness of Kedemoth unto Sihon king of Heshbon with words of peace, saying, Let me pass through thy land: I will go along by the high way, I will neither turn unto the right hand nor to the left. Thou shalt sell me meat for money, that I may eat; and give me water for money, that I may drink: only I will pass through on my feet; (As the children of Esau which dwell in Seir, and the Moabites which dwell in Ar, did unto me;) until I shall pass over Jordan into the land which the LORD our God giveth us.

"But Sihon king of Heshbon would not let us pass by him: for the LORD thy God hardened his spirit, and made his heart obstinate, that he might deliver him into thy hand, as appeareth this day. And the LORD said unto me, Behold, I have begun to give Sihon and his land before thee: begin to possess, that thou mayest inherit his land.

"Then Sihon came out against us, he and all his people, to fight at Jahaz. And the LORD our God delivered him before us; and we smote him, and his sons, and all his people. And we took all his cities at that time, and utterly destroyed the men, and the women, and the little ones, of every city, we left none to remain: Only the cattle we took for a prey unto ourselves, and the spoil of the cities which we took.

"From Aroer, which is by the brink of the river of Arnon, and from the city that is by the river, even unto Gilead, there was not one city too strong for us: the LORD our God delivered all unto us: Only unto the land of the children of Ammon thou camest not, nor unto any place of the river Jabbok, nor unto the cities in the mountains, nor unto whatsoever the LORD our God forbad us. (Deut 2:13-37)

"Ar, the coast of Moab..." is a description of the map's *Arcos*, which is shown on the Moab side of the Amazon-Maranon River, on the coast of the Atlantic Sea.

Another city, which the Bible calls *Aroer*, "which is by the brink of the river of Arnon," appeared to be the city shown on the old map as "Oeiras."

Whether Aroer and Oeiras were two names for the same city was not critical. The Hebrews' Exodus had become a military invasion of Egypt!

Chapter 29

"A dream sees the Exodus"

The Hebrews had taken land in South America. From there, the story in *Numbers* remembers that the Hebrews went to take land from a king called Og, at a city called Edrei and a place called Bashan.

I searched day and night for Edrei and Bashan. Old maps, new maps, ancient history, modern history—I could find nothing of Bashan or Edrei.

The biblical writer said the Hebrews "...turned and went up by the way of Bashan."

Following the description—"up by the way of Bashan"—I looked "up" against the sides of the mountains on the New Orleans map where the Amorites had been, but there was nothing that hinted of the names, Bashan or Edrei.

I had come too far to lose the trail now. Night after night, I pushed my sight over every inch of the eastern side of the South American continent, but I could not find where the Hebrews had gone.

Three weeks after following the Exodus to the banks of the Jabbok River, I was still camped there. Then, on a Sunday morning, I dreamed. There had been no dreams—that I could remember—for a long time.

When I woke from the dream and rose from the bed, I was trembling with chills. I couldn't get warm. The

WHEN ROCKS CRY OUT

dream seemed to show that I was looking on the wrong "side."

I put on the thickest coat I had and began considering the "sides" that the Bible passages had moved the Hebrews to.

"What was it that had sides to it—that the dream was referring to?" My chattering teeth and trembling lips barely got the words out.

I considered the Amazon River, but that water did not fit what the dream had seemed to show. *What did the dream . . . IT'S THE JORDAN! I'm looking on the wrong side of the Jordan!"*

The biblical narrative had said people in the Exodus "went *up* to Bashan." Through the Atlantic Ocean flowed the strong equatorial current called "the Jordan" which ran *down* to South America. So, going "up" to Bashan would take the people of the Exodus to where the equatorial current—the Jordan—was coming from.

In the dream, I was walking toward the sunrise. To go *"up"* the Jordan, toward the sunrise, would take the people of the Exodus to ... the western coast of Africa!

I pulled open the map of western Africa, traced my finger "up" the equatorial current...and THERE THEY WERE!—the biblical cities called *Edrei* and *Bashan.* Modern maps call the two places, Ebrie and Grand Bassam. The names were printed against the shore of the country now being called Ivory Coast.

Most scholars explained that the name Ivory Coast referred to the ivory tusks of elephants. There was a much more significant meaning to that name that had nothing to do with ivory tusks.

I returned to the Scriptures and tested the two West African places against the biblical narratives.

The Hebrews had reached West Africa! Finally, I could follow the people of the Exodus again.

I began reading at a passage in *Numbers*:

"And they turned and went up by the way of Bashan: and Og the king of Bashan went out against them, he, and all his people, to the battle at Edrei. And the LORD said unto Moses, Fear him not: for I have delivered him into thy hand, and all his people, and his land; and thou shalt do to him as thou didst unto Sihon king of the Amorites, which dwelt at Heshbon.

"So they smote him, and his sons, and all his people, until there was none left him alive: and they possessed his land.

"And the children of Israel *set forward*, and pitched in the plains of Moab on this side Jordan by Jericho. And Balak the son of Zippor saw all that Israel had done to the Amorites. And Moab was sore afraid of the people, because they were many: and Moab was distressed because of the children of Israel. And Moab said unto the elders of Midian, Now shall this company lick up all that are round about us, as the ox licketh up the grass of the field. And Balak the son of Zippor was king of the Moabites at that time. He sent messengers therefore unto Balaam the son of Beor to Pethor, which is by the river of the land of the children of his people, to call him, saying, Behold, there is a people come out from Egypt: behold, they cover the face of the earth, and they abide over against me..." (Num 21:33 through Num 22:5)

140

The Hebrews had sent their warriors "up" the equatorial current and had defeated the king called Og in West Africa, at Edrei and Bashan.

After that victory, the Hebrew army "set forward"—traveling *forward* with the water of the equatorial current—and returned to their settlements in South America.

That understanding seemed so simple and obvious, but before the dream unraveled it, that biblical trans-Atlantic passage was fenced with blinding difficulty.

Eventually I perceived the thing that had veiled the route of the Exodus where the Hebrews crossed the sea. I had noticed that biblical narratives used the phrase "*passed over*" when a body of water was crossed:

"And he rose up that night, and took his two wives, and his two women servants, and his eleven sons, and *passed over* the ford Jabbok." (Gen. 32:22)

"So he fled with all that he had; and he rose up, and *passed over* the river, and set his face toward the mount Gilead." (Gen. 31:21)

"I am not worthy of the least of all the mercies, and of all the truth, which thou hast shewed unto thy servant; for with my staff I *passed over* this Jordan; and now I am become two bands." (Gen. 32:10)

Even when the water had been "split," or dammed dry, the phrase "passed over" would still appear.

"And the priests that bare the ark of the covenant of the LORD stood firm on dry ground in the midst of Jordan, and all the Israelites *passed over* on dry ground, until all the people were passed clean over Jordan." (Josh 3:17)

At other times, the "passed over" phrase was the *only* hint that water had been forded:

"And he *passed over* before them, and bowed himself to the ground seven times, until he came near to his brother." (Gen. 33:3)

"And thou shalt write upon them all the words of this law, when thou art *passed over*, that thou mayest go in unto the land which the LORD thy God giveth thee, a land that floweth with milk and honey; as the LORD God of thy fathers hath promised thee." (Deut 27:3)

Curiously, however, when the Hebrews moved across the Atlantic Sea into West Africa, into Ebrie, the *"passed over"* phrase is not used in the texts. In fact, there was *nothing* in those biblical accounts that seemed to show that the Hebrews had crossed water to reach Ebrie. Not only had they crossed *water*, they had crossed the Atlantic *Sea!* Yet, nothing in the texts revealed the sea.

When the Hebrews left the east coast of South America and went across the Atlantic into Africa, the biblical writer (or a later interpreter) did not use the phrase "passed over," but wrote:

"And they turned and *went up* by the way of Bashan: and Og the king of Bashan went out against them, he, and all his people, to the battle at Edrei." (Num 21:33)

"Then we turned, and *went up* the way to Bashan: and Og the king of Bashan came out against us, he and all his people, to battle at Edrei." (Deut 3:1)

The biblical passages then veil the movement of the Hebrews on their return from Africa, by again refusing to allow us to know that a sea was crossed:

142

"And the children of Israel *set forward*, and pitched in the plains of Moab on this side Jordan by Jericho." (Num 22:1)

"And they *departed from* the mountains of Abarim, and pitched in the plains of Moab by Jordan near Jericho." (Num 33:48)

The dream unlocked the movement of the Hebrews into West Africa.

The discovery of famed Jericho was only a glance away.

According to the biblical passages, after returning to South America, the Hebrews camped "in the plains of Moab by Jordan near Jericho." The biblical accounts and the New Orleans map had already made it clear that the land of Moab was on the south side of the Amazon River. Now, the Bible was placing Jericho in this same area, on the south side of the Amazon River.

By stating that Jericho was in Moab and "by Jordan," the biblical narratives had provided a tremendous clue to locating the site of ancient Jericho.

Pulling the New Orleans map before me, I pressed my fingertip against the place where the Amazon River meets the Atlantic Ocean. I traced my finger southward through the Moabite side of the Amazon, passing extremely small, finely printed names on the map. In less than a minute, Jericho was found.

On the New Orleans map, Jerico is shown on the Atlantic shore of Brazil, in the large district that appears to be named for Pharaoh Meriamon Piankhi. The map gave Jerico the surname of "acoara."

The famed Jericho of countless Sunday sermons was found!

One theologian suggested that biblical names on a map of South America could mean that the place on the map was simply named in remembrance of another place.

What he meant was that names of biblical places in South America could have been named in remembrance of the "real" places named in the Scriptures.

I had to smile at the comment.

Not ironically, ancient and antique maps do not show the names of these biblical places in the land now being called the Middle East. But antique and ancient maps do show those biblical names in South America.

In fact it was the absence of maps showing the biblical places that caused archaeologists to pour into the Middle East, to begin digging to try to find where the cities had been. How strange it was that ancient maps showed the biblical names in South America, while ancient maps did not show those names in the other place.

I also knew that the scholars and archaeologists were having an awful time trying to find the biblical cities in the Middle East. In fact, frustration over the past 200 years of searching had grown so troublesome that many of the scholars were proclaiming that the Old Testament "is a myth," because they could not find the route of the Exodus or signs in the dirt that the Old Testament had actually occurred.

With no good sea to place the famed fishing village Capernaum on, they had stood up stones on a waterless place and said an earthquake must have swallowed the sea that Scriptures place Peter's city on.

Imagine the difficulty in attempting to recreate seaside fishing villages and cities along the Atlantic Sea on barren, dry, waterless land in the interior of the Sinai Peninsula.

Their frustration was self-induced. I did not share in it.

I wouldn't have noticed Jericho if I hadn't understood the biblical passages about crossing the Atlantic.

The ocean-crossing biblical key was in hand. This key explained what Scriptures in *Joshua* mean when they state:

"... the Reubenites and the Gadites have received their inheritance, which Moses gave them, *beyond Jordan eastward,* (Josh 13:8)

The tribes called Gad and Reuben settled and claimed land in West Africa, on the *eastern* side of the Atlantic Ocean.

Near the end of the *Joshua* account the writer moves other Hebrew tribes back onto the western side of the Atlantic where they plant city-states that united and became known as "Israel," together with the two and a half "tribes" in West Africa. Because the Gad and Reuben nations were so far from the other nations called Israel, the West African nations were given their own holy temple to worship sacred occasions in. That is why the two calves were set up in the place that Scriptures call "Dan." The "Dan" people of West Africa are still known by that name.

It would be years before I would comprehend the full length of land in the Americas that was called Israel. Finding the city called "Jezreel" was the key to that understanding.

Still, the route of the Exodus was now known. The Exodus began in the Peten region of the Yucatan Peninsula, where Moses had fled to, from Egypt's Thebes. The Exodus moved through Central America, and then it followed the coast of South America to Venezuela. The Hebrews approached Guyana for passage, but were denied. From Kadesh, in Venezuela, the Exodus pressed southward, and entered the poisonous forests of South America. After a troubled journey, the people reached Brazil's Atlantic shore. From Brazil, the Hebrews' Exodus became a military invasion of cities in the Americas and West Africa.

From the time I comprehended the route of the Exodus, more than a year would pass before I would perceive an astounding thing: passages in the Bible actually confirm that the Exodus moved *SOUTHWARD* out of Egypt, not northward, as modern historians claim!

Two passages in *Numbers* come together to show that the Exodus moved southward out of Egypt:

"The standard of the camp of Dan shall be *on the north side* by their armies...." (Num 2:25)

"All they that were numbered in the camp of Dan were an hundred thousand and fifty and seven thousand and six hundred. They shall *go hindmost* with their standards." (Num 2:31)

The Dan people were placed in the most northward position during the march of the Exodus. This northward placement of the Dan tribe was also the "hindmost" position during that long march. When the "hindmost"—or rear—of a migrating group is at the north end of that group, then the front of the group

146

must be at the south end, which means the group is headed southward.

I do not know how this clear biblical declaration of a southward-moving Exodus escaped the perception of the scholars.

It is impossible to reach the land now claiming to be ancient Israel by moving southward out of the Egypt in northeast Africa.

A dream had shown these things. But, how could a dream have known this?

Chapter 30

"The Hyksos and their king, called Saul"

It's easy for me, now, to write that the Hebrews fled out of Egypt, then returned and took Egypt's cities. But when I first perceived that strange about-face, adrenaline rushed through me and stood me up, pulling my eyes from the reading. I had not anticipated that stunning turn of events.

In church sermons that I had heard, the Hebrews had been quiet, mild-mannered, defenseless folk. Somehow, the vicious battles at Edrei and those near the Jabbok River never left an impression in my memory; or the sermons never touched those accounts. Hadn't the Hebrews simply walked around Jericho, and the walls fell down?

That walk at Jericho did not impress upon my young mind that the Hebrews were a merciless, slaughtering army of invaders, ruthless enough to frighten the hardened warriors of Egypt. I certainly did not notice that the Exodus included a Hebrew *army*—600,000 soldiers strong—as some Old Testament passages quietly announced.

"… the LORD said, Bring out the children of Israel from the land of Egypt according to their *armies*." (Exod 6:26).

"But Pharaoh shall not hearken unto you, that I may lay my hand upon Egypt, and bring forth mine *armies*…out of the land of Egypt…." (Exod 7:4)

"And ye shall observe the feast of unleavened bread; for in this selfsame day have I brought your *armies* out of the land of Egypt…" (Exod 12:17)

"And the children of Israel journeyed from Rameses to Succoth, about *six hundred thousand* on foot that were men, beside children." (Exod 12:37)

It was hard to understand how I had not seen these "armies," which were so clearly announced in the biblical writings. But now I understood that these Hebrew armies invaded Egypt and took its cities!

Egypt was the "promised land."

That shocking piece of understanding answered many questions, including the vexing riddle: "Who were the people called 'Hyksos' who invaded and defeated Egypt during Old Testament times?"

The Hyksos were indeed the Hebrews.

Modern biblical scholars reasoned and argued that the Exodus took place during the time of Ramses II. But the autobiography of Moses names Amenemhet I. as the Pharaoh who ruled when Moses fled to Peten. That revelation places Ramses about 700 years after the time of Moses and the Exodus.

If it is true that Pharaoh Amenemhet I died around 1970 BC, then the Exodus left the Yucatan Peninsula about 1940 BC.

Historians, refusing to acknowledge Moses in the Egyptian records, had placed the Hebrews' flight from Egypt hundreds of years later than when it actually occurred. That error did not allow the Hebrews to be the invaders that Egyptian histories called Hyksos.

Manetho, an Egyptian priest, told what Egyptian records said about the Hebrew invasion of Egypt. The Jewish historian Josephus put Manetho's record into his own history, and quoted the Egyptian priest to say:

'There was a king of ours, whose name was Timaus. Under him it came to pass, I know not how, that God was averse to us, and there came, after a surprising manner, men of ignoble birth out of the eastern parts, and had boldness enough to make an expedition into our country, and with ease subdued it by force, yet without our hazarding a battle with them. So when they had gotten those that governed us under their power, they afterwards burnt down our cities, and demolished the temples of the gods, and used all the inhabitants after a most barbarous manner: nay, some they slew, and led their children and their wives into slavery. At length they made one of themselves king, whose name was *SALATIS*; he also lived at Memphis, and made both the upper and lower regions pay tribute, and left garrisons in places that were the most proper for them. He chiefly aimed to secure the eastern parts, as foreseeing that the Assyrians, who had there the greatest power, would be desirous of that kingdom and invade them; and as he found in the Saite (Sethroite) Nomos a city very proper for his purpose, and which lay upon the Bubastic channel, but with regard to a certain theologic notion was called Avaris, this he rebuilt, and made very strong by the walls he built about it, and by a most numerous garrison of two hundred and forty thousand armed men whom he put into it to keep it. Thither Salatis came in summer time, partly to gather his corn and pay his soldiers their wages, and partly to exercise his armed men, and thereby to terrify foreigners. When this man had reigned thirteen years, after him reigned another whose name was Beon for forty-four years; after him reigned another, called Apachnas, thirty-six years and seven months: after him Apophis reigned sixty-one years, and then Jonias fifty years and one month; after all these reigned Assis forty-nine years and two months.

'And these six were the first rulers among them, who were all along making war with the Egyptians, and were very desirous gradually to destroy them to the very roots. This whole nation was styled Hycsos, that is 'Shepherd-kings'; for the first syllable Hyc, according to the sacred dialect denotes a *king*, as is SOS, *a shepherd*—but this according to the ordinary dialect; and of these is compounded HYCSOS: but some say that these people were Arabians. These people whom we have before named *kings*, and called *shepherds* also, and their descendants, kept possession of Egypt five hundred and eleven years.'[lvi]

So spoke an ancient Egyptian priest, who had seen Egypt's records of history.

I saw the name "Salatis" and immediately the Hebrew king Saul stood up in my mind.

Even the second king that the Egyptian priest had named appeared to match what biblical writers had preserved about the second king of the Hebrews, King David, who was said to have ruled for more than 40 years.

There was, however, a problem with the belief that *"Saul"* was *"Salitis."* I had noticed that a Bible passage stated that Saul ruled for 40 years. My body froze when I remembered that Egypt's own record placed Salitis on the throne for only 13 years.

A search through records about Saul showed there was a long-standing controversy about how long Saul actually ruled. It seemed that the ancient record was torn, or worn, where the number of years for Saul's reign was written. That record said that Saul was "one" when he began to rule, and that he ruled for more years after killing another ruler. For the number of years that Saul ruled "as king" after killing the other king, the old record showed the number "2" but a number that was before the "2" was missing from the record.

Scholars could only guess at what number was written before the "2," making it uncertain whether Saul ruled as king for 12, 22, 32, or even 42 years.

I saw an answer to the dilemma. Saul ruled for one year as king of the Hebrews only. After killing the Egyptian king, Saul became a ruler of Egypt, too. He reigned for 12 years as king of a part of Egypt. The Egyptian priest had clearly explained that the Hyksos kings replaced the Egyptian kings and ruled Egypt. Saul's reign as king of the Hebrews for 1 year, then as "king" of Egypt for 12 years, would bring Saul's reign to 13 years, just as the Egyptian priest had seen written in the Egyptian records under the name "Salitis."

Again, this was too simple, and biblical scholars were too educated not to have noticed these things. How had they missed seeing this?

Maybe they hadn't missed it. Maybe they looked a bit deeper into the record and saw the next thing that I saw.

Chapter 31

"Black shepherds take Egypt"

The Egyptian records gave more than the length of reign for each Hyksos ruler; the old carved monuments also showed that the Hyksos had physical features that historians assigned to "Black" Africans.

When I saw those images, I began to understand why modern scholars did not announce Egypt's Sinuhe to be Moses and why the first "shepherd" king, Salatis, had not been recognized as the Hebrew shepherds' first king, Saul.

Wasn't Saul a shepherd? After becoming king, wasn't Saul a shepherd-king? That was the very definition of the name "Hyksos."

Hadn't Saul gone after the animals that were lost from his father's herd? Besides serving as a shepherd for his father's flocks, the Scriptures clearly show Saul was a shepherd even after being crowned king:

"And, behold, Saul came after the herd out of the field ... and he took a yoke of oxen, and hewed them in pieces ..."

The next king of the Hebrews, King David, had been a shepherd, too.

Egyptologist Budge could not suppress his urge to discuss the racial dilemma brought by the ancient Egyptian monuments about these "shepherd kings" who took Egypt's cities:

"The country from which the Hyksos came . . .is unknown. Some Egyptologists consider the Hyksos to be Cushites, and some think they are to be identified with the Accadians; others, again, believe them to be Phoenicians or Semites. The features of the statues that have come down to us which are attributed to the Hyksos, have the following characteristics: The eyes are comparatively small, the nose is broad but aquiline, the cheek bones are prominent and the cheeks thick, the mouth is broad, the lips thick, and the chin protrudes slightly. From these facts some have stated decidedly that the Hyksos cannot have been Semites, but it must be proved that the monuments attributed to the Hyksos were really made by them, before this question can be considered to be definitively disposed of."[lvii]

Five years after seeing Budge's descriptions of these original Hebrews, I found another curious description of the *color* of the original Hebrews. Obadiah Da Bertinoro, a Jewish Rabbi who traveled to the Americas a few years before Columbus had sailed across the Atlantic, described what he determined to be *"descendants"* of the *original* Israelites in a short, clear declaration. The Rabbi wrote:

"I saw two of them...they were black..."

If the Hyksos, or rather Hebrews, were Black Africans (or "Cushites," as Budge calls them) then the obvious question from that is: "Who are the non-Black people in the *modern* Middle East who now claim the ancient name and heritage of the Old Testament Hebrews?"

I have not pursued the origin of the people who now call themselves Jews. It may be possible to understand their origin by researching Josephus' writings in *Against Apion* and biblical narratives about the re-peopling of Israel and Jerusalem, following the Babylonian captivity of Jerusalem's, and Israel's, African inhabitants. The answer, however, could be so explosive that it would rival, in secrecy, Fray Sahagun's *Forbidden Histories*.

Curiously, the Jewish historian Josephus wrote that the name "Jew" was not used until after the Babylonian captivity.

More curious are the ancient debates where Josephus wrote feverishly against classical Greek claims that the "new" inhabitants of Jerusalem and Israel were *not* the Hebrews whose story was recorded in the ancient histories, including the Old Testament narratives. Those Greeks ridiculed Josephus' arguments to the contrary. It seemed that even Josephus' meticulous efforts were no match for the stone proof that shined from the African faces on the ancient monuments in the Americas, and from the ancient records left by Egypt.

Actually, those "Greeks" didn't need the stone images in the Americas to tell them about the Hebrews. Before they were called "Greeks," they were called "Argives."

156

Their secret identity, and origin, of the Argives lay in Scriptures about the place called "Argob." It was another 'forbidden' thing. Mali, Ghana, Nigeria, and Niger should know this secret.

Chapter 32

"Ancient hieroglyphs name cities in the Yucatan Peninsula"

From his military base near Jericho, Joshua sent his warriors to attack a city called *Ai*. That was no small feat, as Ai is located on the Yucatan Peninsula, in the country we now call Belize. The Hebrews had to ply across a thousand miles of Atlantic and Caribbean seas to reach Ai.

But why had Joshua set his heart against Ai?

Biblical history about Abraham could provide an answer to that.

"Now the LORD had said unto Abram, Get thee out of thy country, and from thy kindred, and from thy father's house, unto a land that I will shew thee: ...So Abram departed, as the LORD had spoken unto him... and...went forth to go into the land of Canaan...And Abram passed through the land unto the place of Sichem, unto the plain of Moreh. And the Canaanite was then in the land. And the LORD appeared unto Abram, and said, Unto thy seed will I give this land: and there builded he an altar unto the LORD, who appeared to him. And he removed from thence unto a mountain on the east of Bethel, and pitched his tent, having Bethel on the west, and Hai on the east: and there he builded an altar...."

On modern maps that show ancient Maya cities, the Old Testament city, "Ai," seemed to be the Mayan city called "Ha," or "Altun Ha."

Biblical passages place Ai and Hai "east of Bethel."

The names *Ai* and *Hai* appear to be two Old Testament names for the same city. Clearly, the name "Ai" is embedded in the name "Hai."

There is a major mountain range to the west of the Maya city Altun Ha, but more amazing is the Maya place called "Altar of Sacrifice" that stands between Altun Ha on the east, and the mountain range on the west.

There must have been some important reason why this Maya place was named *"Altar of Sacrifice."* Was this the place where Abraham had built his "altar"? I was not sure.

Still, Joshua's ships had plied the waves of an ocean and seas to reach *Ai.*

Maybe Joshua knew the old traditions about Abraham and this place. Was Joshua going to Ai because that was the place where ancient traditions said Abraham was when the divine promise of land was delivered to him?

Modern maps call this country where Altun Hai is, "Belize." Amazingly, ancient Egyptian writings give this place the same name, calling it—"Bailos."

When modern historians "broke" the code of Egypt's hieroglyphs and began to decipher and publish those writings, they, unwittingly, decoded histories about cities and places in the Americas.

The following is what Brugsch published about the Maya city called *Tikal*, whose pyramids and expansive ruins are located in the south-central region of the Yucatan Peninsula. Brugsch interpreted the Egyptian hieroglyphic name of the city to be *"Thukul."*

"Lying east of the Tanite nome was the eighth, or Sethroite, whose capital bore the name of Pa-Tmu, 'city of Tmu,' the Pithom of the Bible. This town formed the central point of a district, the name of which is of foreign origin, for Thuku, or Succoth, is a Semitic word signifying a 'tent' or 'camp.' This was pasture-land and the property of Pharaoh, and on it the wandering Bedawi of the eastern deserts pitched their tents in order to procure necessary food for their cattle. Here the Israelites first encamped at the time of the Exodus, moving on the second day to a place called Etham, which was either in the country of Succoth or in its close neighbourhood..."[lviii]

Tikal is located in the region called Peten. This is the same "Peten" named in Moses' autobiography. By locating the biblical "Pithom" near to the Mayan city "Tikal," and near to other Mayan cities, Brugsch had,

160

unknowingly, confirmed that Moses had fled to the Yucatan Peninsula!

Brugsch ran into a dead-end while trying to find Tikal and Avaris in the Egypt in northeast Africa. But that was inevitable. Brugsch confessed:

"The gradual silting up of the ancient bed of the river [Nile of Africa] has made the situation of the towns on its banks so difficult to determine, that there is scarcely a hope of finding again the site of the lost city of Avaris."[lix]

"Another town on the east side of the Delta bore the name of Pa-Bailos (Belbeis), the Semitic origin of which is made clear by its evident relationship with the Hebrew, Balas (the large sycomore)."[lx]

Brugsch had published, for modern eyes, the names of several Maya places on the Yucatan Peninsula, including Peten, Becan, Tikal, Altun Hai, and Belize. He was reading from ancient Egyptian hieroglyphic texts!

Chapter 33

"Why a sun stands still, above a promised land"

According to the fourth chapter of *Joshua*, after establishing a colony at Ai, the Hebrews boarded their boats, crossed the "Jordan" and returned to the eastern coast of Brazil, arriving at Gilgal, a town the Hebrews had established near Jericho.

While Egypt was drawing up a plan of counter-attack against the invading Hebrews, one of the Egyptian cities in South America formed an alliance with Joshua. According to the Bible, the alliance between the Hebrews and the Egyptian city, Gibeon, forced Egypt to hasten its counter-attack, to discourage more defections by its cities. Egypt's military answer to the Hebrew invasion is recorded at the 10th chapter of *Joshua*.

Unlike Ai, Gibeon was difficult to locate. One biblical account states that, from Gilgal, it took three days to reach Gibeon, (Josh 9:17). Another Old Testament account suggests that Gibeon could be reached overnight from Gilgal (Josh 10:9).

The biblical narratives had taught me to view them in more than one light. The passage that "seems" to state that Gibeon could be reached overnight could also mean that the Hebrews traveled overnight, *on the last day of the journey*, to surprise Egyptian forces with a night-time attack. Here is that passage:

"So Joshua ascended from Gilgal, he, and all the people of war with him, and all the mighty men of valour. And the LORD said unto Joshua, Fear them not: for I have delivered them into thine hand; there shall not a man of them stand before thee. Joshua therefore came unto them suddenly, and went up from Gilgal all night. And the LORD discomfited them before Israel, and slew them with a great slaughter at Gibeon, and chased them along the way that goeth up to Beth-horon, and smote them to Azekah, and unto Makkedah." (Josh 10:7-10)

There *could* be one quiet, but very significant biblical clue to finding Gibeon. It is a curious passage that was inserted in the account of the battle at Gibeon:

"And the sun stood still, and the moon stayed, until the people had avenged themselves upon their enemies. Is not this written in the book of Jasher? So the sun stood still in the midst of heaven, and hasted not to go down about a whole day." (Josh 10:13)

There have been many interpretations of how this sun could *stand still* for *"a whole day."*

There is one answer, or one explanation, which was not available to scholars who thought the Old Testament events had happened in the Middle East region north of Africa. The Tropic of Capricorn stretches across the southern portion of Brazil. If Joshua had reached some town that was situated along or near the Tropic of

Capricorn, then the battle at Gibeon could have witnessed a sun that "stood still" for "about a whole day."

The Tropic of Capricorn is the place where the sun annually *appears* to stop moving southward, before seeming to turn and move north again. During this "winter solstice," the sun seems to pause, for about a day, before it heads back to the north. The very name "solstice" means "sun stand still." It may be that Gibeon will be found near, or along, the Tropic of Capricorn in South America.

The location of Gibeon was a thorn pricking at my understanding, but the most famed city of the ancient world was shimmering through the foliage of South America. It was time to visit *Jerusalem*.

But, first, I wanted to map where the other 10 tribes of Israel had set up their kingdoms.

Chapter 34

"Joshua places Israel in Africa, Central America"

Near the end of Joshua's military conquests, a record was made of lands the Hebrews had won and kings the Hebrews had defeated. That record is given in *Joshua*, at the 12th chapter.

Joshua, or whoever was the writer of the narrative called *Joshua*, seems to have composed the record while being somewhere on the Yucatan Peninsula, or in Central America, since both Africa *and* South America are described as being on "the other side Jordan." The "Jordan," as discussed earlier, was the name given to the equatorial current that runs from West Africa to South America, then along the shores of South America and past the Yucatan Peninsula.

The *Joshua* narratives also provide 'directionals' that pointed to where the Hebrew lands were located. When Hebrew territories in Africa, or lands on the *eastern* shore of South America, were mentioned, there was this directional:

"... on the other side Jordan *eastward.*" (Josh 13:27)

For lands that the Hebrews had taken in Central America, the Scriptures would show those kingdoms to be *"on the west"* of the sea:

"And these are the kings of the country which Joshua and the children of Israel smote *on this side Jordan on the west*...which Joshua gave unto the tribes of Israel for a possession according to their divisions...." (Josh 12:7)

The invasion and capture of Egypt's cities in the Americas, launched during the time of Joshua, eventually carved out an empire that included regions in Mexico, Central America, South America and West Africa.

Descendants of Abraham's descendant "Jair" were among the "two and a half tribes" settled in West Africa. It may be that this "Jair" is the reason Niger (Ni-Jair) and Nigeria (Ni-Jair-ia) have *those* names.

I saw several astonishing records carved on ancient monuments and temples in the Americas about King David and other people famed in the Bible. But a detour to the monuments about David would have to wait for another day.

Ancient writings explain that David took his band of warriors to a southern region that Old Testament narratives call "Hebron." That meant David had reached Bolivia, in South America. Nearby, on the floor of Lake Titicaca lay the ruins of Sodom and Gomorra.

David, the shepherd-turned-king, had gotten into position to pounce on one of the greatest and strongest capital cities of ancient Egypt—a city called *Jerusalem*!

166

Chapter 35

"Enoch's city is not Thebes"

I couldn't remember which piece of understanding was the first to uncover the city in South America that had been ancient Jerusalem.

I did remember that I had written a note to my memory that ancient writers called Jerusalem "the navel of the world." When I identified the city in the Americas that was ancient Jerusalem, the oldest traditions at that city continued to remember that the city was "the navel of the world."

More astounding were ancient traditions left by Egypt in this South American city that remembered extraordinary details about King David's life and his decisions. Just as stunning were ancient South American traditions that told where David retired to, after his son Absalom had driven David from the throne.

When I saw the place in Central America where those traditions said David had gone to live out his life, there were the ancient steles, showing the actual face of David, Saul, Samuel, and Solomon. Written on these steles were events recorded in the Old Testament about David. There was one additional, stunning kind of information: the steles showed the actual *dates* for famed events that had happened in David's life, including the date of

David's birth and the date this king died! But Jerusalem was waiting.

It would be unnecessarily cumbersome to unfold all the things that made it clear which city in the Americas had been Egypt's Jerusalem.

What follows are some of the things that helped me recognize the biblical city where David had ruled, and where Christ had taught, prayed and was killed.

For most of ancient Egypt's history, two cities— Memphis and Thebes—had served alternately as the national capital of this empire, which had been built by uniting kingdoms into one nation. A city in the Yucatan Peninsula had also served as an ancient capital of Egypt, but Memphis and Thebes were the two most enduring capitals.

One of these two capital cities—Memphis or Thebes—was going to be the fortressed city that the Bible called *"Jerusalem."*

Hebrews had taken possession of Memphis at least as early as the time of Saul, according to the Egyptian priest Manetho.

I could not, however, find the account that showed Hebrews taking Egypt's other powerful capital, Thebes.

Further, I had never heard a theologian even speak of Thebes as being mentioned in the Scriptures. I had, however, read that the biblical city called *"No"* was thought to be Egypt's Thebes.

"No" was not Thebes. "No" was Memphis, which was still called *"Te-NO' tit-lan"* (Tenochtitlan) when Cortes arrived at that city in 1519.

This name, "No," was taken from the name, "Enoch." I understood the old writings well enough to

168

know that this place was where Cain had built a city and named it for "Enoch," Cain's son. That would explain why the city on the island was known as "Tenochtitlan."

"And Cain knew his wife; and she conceived, and bare Enoch and he builded a city, and called the name of the city, after the name of his son, Enoch." (Gen. 4:17)

This island—called Enoch, Tenochtitlan and Memphis—is the first city named in the Old Testament.

It is that island, and its city, that is meant by biblical Scriptures that mention "No," including this description:

"Art thou better than populous No, that was situated among the rivers, that had the waters round about it, whose rampart was the sea, and her wall was from the sea?" (Nahum: 3:8)

Interpreters of the biblical narratives mistakenly called the great lakes that surrounded this island, a *"sea."* It was a common mistake made by translators who had to determine which kind of water was meant by an ancient symbol that denoted bodies of water. Often, the same symbol could mean river, lake, or other bodies of water.

When I saw the ruins of ancient Egypt's Thebes, in South America, the city did not fit biblical descriptions given for the city called "No." There had been no "sea" serving as that city's "rampart" as Scriptures described. Egypt's Thebes, in South America, was hundreds of miles from the sea.

However, Egypt's Memphis (Tenochtitlan) did fulfill biblical descriptions for "No," with the waters of the great lakes serving as defensive "ramparts," or walls, against attacks, as the Piankhi Stele had shown.

Still, if the Scriptures' "*No*" was the biblical name for Memphis, where in the Bible was the great Egyptian capital city called Thebes? And why didn't the Egyptian histories mention "Jerusalem."

Chapter 36

"As above, so below"

Sermons that I had heard had not given me the understanding that Jerusalem was an Egyptian city, though it certainly was. Old Testament passages made it clear that Jerusalem was a *leading* Egyptian city.

In the biblical narratives, when the Hebrew armies pressed their attack deep into South America—at Gibeon—Egypt assembled warriors from several of its important city-states and went to check the invasion. It was strange that the Bible did not name Thebes as one of the Egyptian cities that went out to face Joshua, especially since Thebes was the most powerful Egyptian city in the southern region of Egypt's empire. A major attack on Egypt's South American provinces should have produced a response from Thebes. Instead, the Egyptian city that led the counter-attack against the Hebrews was… *"Jerusalem"*:

"Adoni-zedek *king of Jerusalem sent unto* Hoham king of Hebron, and unto Piram king of Jarmuth, and unto Japhia king of Lachish, and unto Debir king of Eglon, saying, Come up unto me, and help me, that we may smite Gibeon: for it hath made peace with Joshua and with the children of Israel. Therefore the five kings of the Amorites, the king of Jerusalem, the king of Hebron, the king of Jarmuth, the king of Lachish, the king of Eglon, gathered themselves together, and went up, they and all their hosts, and encamped before Gibeon, and made war against it." (Josh: 10:3-5)

It didn't make sense that none of the most powerful cities of ancient Egypt were named during this Hebrew attack on Egypt.

I could feel Jerusalem trying to show itself. I had thought to uncover this hidden city with my intellect, as though that had been the thing that had brought me this far, but my intellect was smothering my instincts.

I closed the voices of every page that lay open around me and walked out into the night. The three clear stars at Orion's waist were still leaning against the black sky. They had moved from the eastern horizon into the height where a noon sun would hang. The single dim streetlight a half-block away allowed the stars and black sky to be my dark woods that night. I sat down on the hard steps of the porch, tilted my eyes toward the stars and waited for a cool night breeze to visit.

The winds came, streamed across me and then melted toward the south. Curiously, thin wisps of clouds moved slowly in the opposite direction, toward the north, sailing across Orion. The flotilla of clouds, moving the wrong way, held my gaze against Orion until the clouds had crossed the entire length of the man. I had just begun to notice the red and blue tints in the stars' lights when something stood up in my understanding.

I wheeled on my palms and half-crawled, half-ran, up the brick stairs, bursting into the room that was littered with stacks of books that reached to my knees.

I turned slowly in the middle of the room, urging my thoughts to recall which books, which pages, held the pieces of the secret that I had just been shown. I had to hurry: understanding had sometimes faded before I could burn it into my memory. I didn't want to lose any piece of the comprehension that had suddenly assembled itself inside of me.

I pulled out the faded green book that held Josephus' *Histories* then I turned several columns of books until I found the translations of the ancient Egyptian inscriptions.

Next, my eyes found the mustard colored cover of the one book that would pull the whole thing together. It was the mustard colored book that held the key to unlocking the secret of Jerusalem. But, first, I had to find the other pieces.

While staring at Orion, it had suddenly become clear to me that an ancient city on the Yucatan Peninsula seemed to have designed in the likeness of the Orion constellation. When I found the drawings of the Yucatan city, Chichen Itza, there was the image of Orion, with three temples across the "waist" of the city to show the three stars at the waist of Orion. A paved street formed the raised right arm of Orion, while some ruined structures mimicked a weapon stretched high in his hand. A very large round well at the end of a straight street produced the likeness of a head and neck for the man known as Orion.

I saw another design formed at Chichen Itza, but I hold that understanding for another effort.

I pushed back from the mapped layouts of Chichen Itza and remembered how the lakes of Memphis were dug out to form the shape of a crocodile—the totem spirit of Memphis.

"Wouldn't the Egyptians have built the capital in Upper Egypt in the image of its totem, like they had done at Memphis? And if they had designed Thebes in the likeness of its totem, then what was the totem of Thebes?"

Chapter 37

"City of the hidden name"

Egyptians did not call their city "Thebes." The Greeks gave that name to the city.

Whatever name the Egyptians first gave to the city, they wrote that this capital was in "Upper Egypt," and that it was called the throne of Heru. Heru was one of ancient Egypt's earliest Pharaohs and he was so famed in antiquity that his name gave us the word "hero."

Using its hieroglyphics, Egypt wrote the name "Heru" by drawing the profile of a standing hawk. But when I checked the hieroglyphs for the symbol used to write the name Thebes, the likeness of a strange animal was drawn, which scholars could not identify.

They could not identify the animal because they did not know that this city was built in Peru. The animal shown with this city's name is the square-eared llama of South America.

Since the lakes around Memphis were designed to show a crocodile, would the ruins of Thebes-Jerusalem show the outline of a llama?

I considered that possibility, but I remembered something. Egypt's priests had let out a secret about this city. The scribes wrote that this capital city was:

"the city of the hidden name"

The old writings revealed another secret: a temple at Thebes was called:

"the eye of Re, mistress of temples"

I believed these were secret codes to what was designed in the layout of the city. Scholars had long ago interpreted that the Egyptians referred to the man, Heru, as *"Re."* The code in the hieroglyphs seemed to say that the city was built in the likeness of Heru, and that a temple was built where Heru's eye would normally be.

Would the ancient Egyptians have been so ingenuous that they would build a city and make it show its name in its layout?

If Thebes was not built in the shape of a llama, then maybe it would be in the shape of a hawk, and maybe the structure serving as a temple would be positioned where the eye of the hawk would be.

I turned through the pages of the mustard colored book, examining the layouts of the ancient cities of South America. My fingers froze on illustrations of Cuzco!

The walls, streets, rivers and canals of Cuzco formed a clear image of the profile of a hawk—the Egyptian hieroglyphic for the word, "Heru." I looked closer at the drawings. There were the foundation stones from what had been a round temple, and the stones were forming the eye of the hawk!

I couldn't celebrate: Something was igniting urgency in me. The pieces were flying together. My heart was pounding.

When Josephus penned his important history, *Antiquities of the Jews,* he shared an interesting thing about ancient Jerusalem:

"When David had cast the Jebusites out of the citadel, he also rebuilt Jerusalem, and named it *The City of David,* and abode there all the time of his reign; but for the time that he reigned over the tribe of Judah only in Hebron, it was seven years and six months. Now when he had chosen Jerusalem to be his royal city, his affairs did more and more prosper, by the providence of God, who took care that they should improve, and be augmented. Hiram also, the king of the Tyrians, sent ambassadors to him , and made a league of mutual friendship and assistance with him. He also sent him presents, cedar-trees, and mechanics, and men skillful in building and architecture, that they might build him a royal palace at Jerusalem. Now David made buildings round about the lower city: he also joined the citadel to it, and made it one body; and when he had encompassed all with walls, he appointed Joab to take care of them. It was David, therefore, who first cast the Jebusites out of Jerusalem, and called it by his own name, *The City of David*: for under our forefather Abraham it was called (Salem, or) Solyma; but after that time, some say that Homer mentions it by that name of Solyma, [for he named the temple Solyma, according to the Hebrew language, which denotes security.]"[lxi]

In the footnote about the name Jerusalem, an editor wrote, "Some copies of Josephus have here Solyma, or Salem; and others Hierosolyma, or Jerusalem. The latter best agree to what Josephus says elsewhere, that this city was called Solyma, or Salem, before the days of

177

Melchisedec, but was by him called Hierosolyma, or Jerusalem."[lxii]

That simple footnote, showing that "Jerusalem" was also "Hierosolyma," helped unlock the secret location of Jerusalem in the Americas.

Greek writers preferred using the name *Horus* and *Hiero* instead of *Heru*. So, *Heru, Horus* and *Hiero*, all, refer to the ancient deified Pharaoh that the Egyptians called Heru.

Rome's Julius Caesar explained in his *Gallic Wars* that the word *solym* was taken from the word "sol" which means sun.

Combining pieces of understanding from the biblical narratives, from the footnote in Josephus, from the notes of Julius Caesar, and from the Egyptian histories, the meaning of the name "Jerusalem" was uncovered.

The biblical city called Jerusalem was the Egyptian capital city named for Heru, the deified Egyptian king whose memory was to be kept alive by using the daily presence of the sun to commemorate him. Jerusalem's name was more properly, "Heru-solym," from Heru and the sun.

If that is offensive to some, I can only say, "Wait until you comprehend the meaning of the biblical writing called *Revelation* where it reveals Egypt's great founder "Amen" (Rev. 3:14). That passage uncovers the meaning of events in *Genesis* and the Old Testament, generally. Those coded Scriptures are called *Revelation* for a reason.

Now I understood why the ancient hieroglyphs described the man Amen to be "far seeing." It was written that Amen had built Heru's city to last "for a million years." Egypt's design of Jerusalem and the

178

"hidden name" that Egypt placed in that design had, so far, lasted for more than 17,000 years.

The gigantic walls and foundations at Cuzco had even survived Spain's massive destruction of *"The Forbidden Histories."* The conquistadors had no way to fly above the city, so they could not see what Egypt had done. They could not see the name "Heru" being spelled out by the city's walls and streets and other structures.

Jerusalem was built with its stones crying out the city's name. Here was the Horus throne of Upper Egypt, sitting in a valley nearly 12,000 feet above the sea. It was clear why the hieroglyphs described this city as being in *"Upper Egypt."*

More important, it could finally be understood what was meant by biblical narratives that warned: Jerusalem will come down from a mountain.

There was one dilemma that needed resolving. The Bentresh Stele showed "Thebes" to be so far away that 17 months was needed to travel between Beken, in the Yucatan, and the Thebes where Ramses was. Moses had reached South America, from the Yucatan, in less than 2 months; so the need for 17 months of travel to reach Peru from Beken in the Yucatan seemed to rule out Peru as being the site for Thebes (Jerusalem).

That dilemma was answered by other Egyptian hieroglyphics, which clarify that there were actually two Egyptian cities called Thebes. One Thebes was called *"Thebes of the West."* I had to remember that the Egyptian hieroglyphic texts had called the Americas *"The South Land and the North Land,"* just as we still call those two continents "South America" and "North America."

Egypt also called the Americas, *"The Two Lands."* The ancient hieroglyphics place *"Thebes of the West"* in *"the Two Lands,"* in the Americas.

Chapter 38

"Jerusalem: Bible calls it Thebes"

I wrote earlier that Thebes was not mentioned in the Old Testament accounts and that preachers confirmed that. Yet, there are *two* mentions of Egypt's Thebes in the Old Testament.

When I saw "Thebes" in the Old Testament, I could not understand how I had missed seeing it earlier. David received fame for capturing this city (under its names, Jerusalem and Jebusi), but, actually, a Hebrew army led by Abimelech had captured the city before the time of David. However, a well-dropped stone won that city back for Egypt, according to the narrative called *Judges*:

"Then went Abimelech to *Thebez*, and encamped against Thebez, and took it. But there was a strong tower within the city, and thither fled all the men and women, and all they of the city, and shut it to them, and gat them up to the top of the tower. And Abimelech came unto the tower, and fought against it, and went hard unto the door of the tower to burn it with fire. And a certain woman cast a piece of a millstone upon Abimelech's head, and all to brake his skull. Then he called hastily unto the young man his armourbearer, and said unto him, Draw thy sword, and slay me, that men say not of me, A woman slew him. And his young man thrust him through, and he died. And when the men of Israel saw that Abimelech was dead, they departed every man unto his place." (Judges: 9:50-55)

In that passage, the "*s*" in Thebes has been replaced with the letter "*z*". "Thebe*s*" became "Thebe*z*," and the great Egyptian capital city disappeared from the Bible.

As with many names that I saw during the search, only a slight change was made to disguise the Egyptian presence. The disguise draped over Thebes was so thin it was like hiding an elephant under a silk scarf, yet the disguise had effectively hidden the city from the eyes of the world for over 500 years.

Josephus removed the veil from the Bible's "Thebez." In a passage about the death of Bathsheba's husband, Uriah, Josephus wrote:

"...Joab sent messengers to [David], and ordered them to tell him that he did what he could to take the city soon; but that as they made an assault on the wall, they had been forced to retire with great loss; and bade them, if they saw the king was angry at it, to add this, that Uriah was slain also. When the king had heard this of the messengers, he took it heinously, and said that they did wrong when they assaulted the wall, whereas they ought, by undermining and other stratagems of war, to endeavour the taking of the city, especially when they had before their eyes the example of Abimelech, the son of Gideon, who would needs take the tower in *Thebes* by force, and was killed by a large stone thrown at him by an old woman..."[lxiii]

The biblical "Thebez" is shown by Josephus to be "Thebes."

If scholars would now argue that there was another city named Thebez, with massive walls and a great citadel, they must first stand up such an imaginary city, which hopefully will be more visible than the Heliopolis and Memphis that have been conjured into existence.

When I looked at the hieroglyphs that named the ancient districts of Upper Egypt, one hieroglyph kept appearing: the image of the hawk enclosed within a square. This square with the opening was the Egyptian symbol for the word *"Per,"* meaning "house," or "temple"; and the hawk symbol, as stated earlier, meant *"Heru."* The Egyptian expression was saying, *"Per Heru,"* the "house (or temple) of Heru," which became the abbreviated name *"Peru."*

Egyptologist Brugsch gave a clue to this when he wrote, "The [Egyptian] sovereign bears the official title of 'King of Upper and Lower Country;' he is also called Per-ao . . . better known, perhaps, under the Hebrew equivalent of Pharaoh."[lxiv]

The Egyptian hieroglyphics had called out the name of South America's *"Peru"* right in front of my eyes, and I had not understood the call.

Chapter 39

"City of David: Zion on the north"

There are several ancient accounts that mention David's fortress (or "citadel"), which stood above—*and on the north side of*—the main city called Jerusalem and Thebes.

First, the passage from the Josephus histories:

"When David had cast the Jebusites out of the *citadel*, he also rebuilt Jerusalem, and named it *The City of David*, and abode there all the time of his reign..."[lxv]

Then, the biblical passages are pressed into place:

"And the king and his men went to Jerusalem unto the Jebusites, the inhabitants of the land...David took the *strong hold of Zion: the same is the city of David*...So David dwelt in the fort, and called it the city of David." (2Sam: 5-9)

"Beautiful for situation, the joy of the whole earth, is *mount Zion, on the sides of the north*, the city of the great King." (Ps: 48:2)

These biblical descriptions clearly locate the fortress called Zion — the City of David — on the *north* side of the lower city of Jerusalem.

184

Curiously, archaeologists and modern scholars ignored these Old Testament descriptions, until the first edition of this book was published. After that publication, efforts began in the Middle East to find David's city on the north side of *that* Jerusalem.

Scholars knew ancient histories place the City of David on a raised spur of rock. But because there is no such spur against the northern side of the place now being called Jerusalem, scholars had pointed to a hill south of that city and labeled it *"the city of David."*

In Peru, the raised mount that once shouldered the City of David has a name and a history. Peruvian traditions give the name "Sacsahuaman" to that mount that was once called Zion. If you pronounce "Sacsahuaman" as some tour guides instruct you ("sexy woman"), you may never comprehend that it is the Egyptian deity "Amen" whose name was given to this sacred hill.

Native Peruvian history about Sacsahuaman includes the important tradition that this hill was both "fortress" and "temple."

The Peruvian tradition that this mountain fortress served as the burial place for kings is confirmed by biblical passages that speak of burials at this city:

"So David slept with his fathers, and was *buried in the city of David*." (1Kgs:2:10)

"… Jehoiada waxed old, and was full of days when he died; an hundred and thirty years old was he when he died. And they *buried him in the city of David among the kings*." (2Chron: 24:15-16)

"[Ahaziah the king of Judah]...his servants carried him in a chariot to Jerusalem, and *buried him in his sepulchre with his fathers in the city of David.*" (2Kgs :9:28)

Another biblical passage places a "pool" near David's sepulcher in the fortress:

"After him repaired Nehemiah the son of Azbuk ... unto the place over against the sepulchres of David, and to the *pool* that was made, and unto the house of the mighty." (Neh: 3:16)

Among the ruins of Sacsahuaman are those "pools" mentioned in the Old Testament.

There is something else that shows Cuzco and its northern fortress to be the Jerusalem of King David that archaeologists say is "missing" in the Middle East. Cuzco has a canal that runs *straight,* and on the *west side,* of the mountain fortress that was Zion. The Old Testament mentions that canal:

"This same Hezekiah also stopped the upper watercourse of Gihon, and brought it *straight* down to the west side of the city of David. ..." (2Chron: 32:30)

Another biblical passage clarifies that this watercourse was a canal, or "conduit":

"And the rest of the acts of Hezekiah, and all his might, and how he made a pool, and a *conduit,* and brought water into the city, are they not written in the book of the chronicles of the kings of Judah?" (2Kgs:20:20)

Back on the other side of the world from Peru, scholars point to a twisting underground tunnel at the modern Jerusalem and call that tunnel the Hezekiah Canal. That tunnel fails to match the clear biblical descriptions of it. That canal is not "straight" and it does not run to the *west side of the city of David.*

The canal at Cuzco is the canal described in the biblical writings about Hezekiah.

For any skeptic who prefers to doubt the biblical placement of Zion on the northern side of Jerusalem, there is the extraordinary clarification provided by an account from the mid-13th century. It was written by the Jewish traveler, Rabbi Jacob, "the messenger of Rabbi Jechiel of Paris." He wrote:

"To-day Jerusalem lies to the north-west of the Temple Mount, not as it used to be, on the south of the Temple Mount as it is said in Ezekiel xl, 2. 'The frame of a city on the South,' and in Psalms xlviii, 3, 'Mount Zion on the sides of the north ... '"

It is the ancient city in Peru, and not the later city in the Middle East, that fits the biblical, and other ancient, descriptions of Jerusalem. To cement that truth as fact, I now reveal what the ancient writers called "the Millo."

Chapter 40

"Jerusalem's famed fortress called 'The Millo'"

"The Millo . . . a rampart consisting of two walls with the space between them filled in; The name of the citadel of Shechem. The Millo at Jerusalem was some kind of fortification ... The definite article before Millo indicates that it was a well-known fortress, probably one that had been built by the Jebusites ..."

That definition of "the Millo" is from the 1916 edition of *The People's Bible Encyclopedia.*

Archaeologists and scholars have never found any remains of "the Millo" in the Middle East. That was inevitable, as the walls of the famed Millo still stand at the Jerusalem that was built by Egypt, in Peru.

"The Millo" was probably the most astonishing and unique walled fortress ever built by ancient Egypt. Finding the Millo—the Egyptian fortress that was taken by David—would show, once and for all, which city was truly the Jerusalem of Adam, Egypt, King David and Christ.

Protecting the north side of Peru's Cuzco are three monumental zigzagging walls so cleverly designed that they are practically impenetrable. The triple walls rise in successive stages and are made of finished boulders, some of which are as great as 5 meters high. Earth fills the space between the walls, forming terraces for soldiers to stand on, to protect the preceding terrace and wall below. The earth between the walls made it almost impossible to knock down the walls.

The stones in the walls are so astonishingly massive and so extraordinarily constructed that these walls were sometimes mentioned with the other Wonders of the Ancient World.

Seeing these cyclopean walls at Cuzo-Jerusalem allows comprehension of the strange biblical passage at 2 Sam. 5:6, which mentions placing *blind* and *lame* people on the walls:

"And the king and his men went to Jerusalem unto the Jebusites, the inhabitants of the land: which spake unto David, saying, Except thou take away the blind and the lame, thou shalt not come in hither ..."

The historian Josephus clarifies the extraordinary meaning of placing *blind* and *lame* persons on the walls of this famed fortress:

"Now the Jebusites, who were the inhabitants of Jerusalem, and were by extraction Canaanites, shut their gates, and placed the blind, and the lame, and all their maimed persons, upon the wall, in way of derision of the king, and said that the very lame themselves would hinder his entrance into it. This they did out of contempt of his power, and as depending on the strength of their walls." (*Antiquities of the Jews*, Book VII, Chapter III, sect. 1)

Josephus explains further, saying that David, indeed, could not take the walled fortress in Peru. Instead, David took the main city of Jerusalem that lay beneath the hilltop fortress:

"So he took the lower city by force, but the citadel held out still."

Finally, David offered a prize for the warrior who could get past the earthen terraces between the walls of the Millo and reach the fortress on top of the hill:

"And David said on that day, Whosoever getteth up to the gutter, and smiteth the Jebusites, and the lame and blind ... he shall be chief and captain ..." (2 Sam. 5:8)

Again, Josephus clarifies the curious "gutter" in that verse:

"...the king ... promised that he who should first go over the *ditches that were beneath the citadel*, and should ascend to the citadel itself and take it, should have the command of the entire people conferred upon him ..."

Such was the fortress and the gigantic walled terraces that the ancient narratives call "the Millo."

How fortunate, that the famed walls of the Millo still stand to serve as a staunch witness to the truth of where ancient Egypt had built its capital city called Jerusalem.

This Millo is also shown in a carved scene inside the temple called Medinet Habu in the second Egypt, in northeast Africa.

Failing to comprehend that Ramses' was attacking Egypt's own Thebes-Jerusalem, Breasted interpreted the Medinet Habu scene to be describing an Egyptian attack on a "Syrian" fortress, which Breasted presumed to be located somewhere north of Africa.

Breasted wrote this about the scene:

"The king assaults a Syrian fortress on foot; he has left his chariot, and shoots with the bow as he advances … the *fortress rises in four successive battlements to a lofty citadel or tower in the middle*, from which waves a triangular banner. Here stands the chief and his companions. The walls are manned with bearded Semites, one of whom offers incense to Ramses from the lowest battlement."[lxvi]

The hieroglyphic inscriptions carved beside the fortress explain that the fortress, under attack by Ramses, belonged to the Amorites. Breasted interpreted the name of the people to be "Amor," but indicated that he could not make out the last letters in the name. The ending must have had the same meaning as the suffix *"ite"* that the Bible places on names such as "Amorite."

I knew there were native Peruvian people whose traditions say they are descendants of a people called "Amurru." But more important, I remembered biblical narratives that relate Jerusalem to the names "Amor" and "Amorite," written on the temple in Africa. The biblical narratives tell us:

"Therefore the five kings of the *Amorites*, the king of *Jerusalem*, the king of Hebron, the king of Jarmuth, the king of Lachish, the king of Eglon, gathered themselves together, and went up, they and all their hosts, and encamped before Gibeon, and made war against it."(Joshua10:5)

And;

"…Thus saith the Lord GOD unto *Jerusalem*; Thy birth and thy nativity is of the land of Canaan; thy father was an *Amorite*, and thy mother an Hittite." (Ezekiel 16:3)

The Amorite piece of the puzzle was fitted into place.

I was not concerned that Breasted called the soldiers on the terraced walls, "Semites." Breasted and other historians frequently used that term to mean any number of kinds of people, including Black Africans.

They also frequently substituted the word "Libyan" as a name for people that the hieroglyphs called "T-h-n-w." When race is drained from scholarship, historians will recognize "T-h-n-w" to mean the Tehenu people of West Africa.[lxvii]

Likewise, another Egyptian term, "Nahasu," was discarded by several Egyptologists and replaced by the word "Negro." An Egyptologist explained:

"The great mixture of tribes who had their homes in the wide regions of the Upper Nile...have on the monuments the common name of Nahasu. From the representations of them we recognize the ancestors of the negro race."

I didn't have to worry about Breasted's "Semite" description because on the Medinet Habu temple the scene showing "the Millo" shows the kind of men being taken as captives from that Jerusalem. Breasted described these men to be four Black Africans, two "Libyan" Africans and one "lost image." Breasted clarified that the Egyptian hieroglyphics describe the first Black African figure in the drawing to be *"the chief of Kush the wretched."*

Kush was one more name for Peru's Cuzco, which was often written as *"Cusco"* on early maps of South America. *Kush* became *"KUSH-co."*

192

The African pointed out by Breasted to be the *"chief of Kush"* was the king of the city that was called at different times; Jerusalem, Thebes, Kush and Cusco.

There was one final thought: The Millo is still standing. So, wouldn't travelers to Jerusalem during the Middle Ages have seen the Millo in Peru? Wouldn't they have written about those monumental walls?

I found the answer in a book called, *The Itinerary of Benjamin of Tudela: Travels in the Middle Ages.*

When Benjamin approached Jerusalem, he wrote this:

"From thence it is three parasangs to Jerusalem, which is a small city, fortified by three walls."[lxviii]

Months later, I found other accounts of these great triple walls at Jerusalem. For some reason, I had failed to consider that Josephus would have left an account of the walls. When I searched his writings, the curiously designed triple walls of Jerusalem, in Peru, came into view there, too. Josephus wrote:

"The city of Jerusalem was fortified with three walls on such parts as were not encompassed with unpassable valleys; for in such places it had but one wall."[lxix]

The "passable" plain stretches out on the north side of Cuzco-Jerusalem, where the "three" great stone walls of the Millo were built to protect against an attack coming across that plain.

Certainly, the "unpassable valleys" that Josephus mentioned are obvious at Cuzco; and the ancient "one wall" that protected the lower city of Cuzco-Jerusalem was well known and had been mapped.

The Jerusalem puzzle had come together, around the famed "Millo" of the Old Testament. Then, something fortunate happened.

Driving from Dallas, I decided to visit a library that was along the route. I asked the Special Collections librarian if they had antique maps of ancient Jerusalem, and they did.

There were two illustrations: one showed the layout of Jerusalem during the Middle Ages; and the other drawing depicted the interior of a temple at Jerusalem during that same era. The maps had been brought to America by French colonists who settled at Dallas.

What I saw on that old layout of Jerusalem stunned me. The map showed three monumental zigzagging walls at the northern end of the city. Here were the famed zigzagging walls of Cuzco *on an early map of the city called Jerusalem!*

Not only did the map show the unique triple walls, it also identified other ruins on that hill at Cuzco, including the temple-fortress called Zion and David's sepulcher! The librarian gave me copies of the two maps.

Back home, I sat quietly, shaking my head. After years of sifting through the stones of America and Egypt, the picture of ancient Jerusalem, standing in a mountain in South America, lay in plain view on my table.

Finally, the meaning of the prayer—which had said the search was not about Egypt, and which seemed to have come so long ago—became clear. The Jerusalem that Egypt built, the city coveted and ruled by David, the city whose temple Christ said would be wiped away, has fulfilled the biblical prophecy about it. And the biblical narratives prophesied that Jerusalem would come down out of a mountain. And that prophecy has now issued fruit.

What kind of strange "miracle" was this: that a city as great as Egypt's Jerusalem could be found in a mountain in South America, when few even knew biblical Jerusalem was lost?

Maybe it could show that God is still with us, doing impossible things—to show us He still can, and to show us He still cares.

They had hidden Christ's Jerusalem well, but who can really hide a thing from God?

In the 12 years since I got these things, there have been countless days and nights when I have found myself on my knees, leaning on the palms of my hands, in the mud of tears. I do not feel the sting of arrows thrown at me from all around. The pain I feel, the crippling blows that drop me into the mud, are the arrows slung from within me—from the seemingly blind bowmen who wear the helmet of fate, and faith.

But even in those threatening storms, with hands sinking into blackened mud, and knees being engulfed by dividing clay, my soul asks the question: "What means the thing, when God whispers down and names a babe at birth with the name of the city that God allows him to find? For 'Horace' is 'Horus,' and 'Horus' is 'Heru,' and 'Heru' is Jerusalem."

And then, sinking, and with the noise of thunder all around me, I remember, "Be peaceful, all things are in my hand."

Cebri.

Works Cited

[i] Margreet Steiner, "It's Not There: Archaeology Proves a Negative," *Biblical Archaeology Review,* July/August 1998: pp 26, 27

[ii] Nadav Na'Aman, "It is There: Ancient Texts Prove It," *Biblical Archaeology Review,* July/August 1998: pp 42, 44

[iii] Hernando Cortes, *Five Letters of Cortes to the Emperor*, trans J. Bayard Morris (New York: W.W. Norton and Co., Inc., 1991) pp 70-71

[iv] Francisco Lopez de Gomara, *Cortes: The Life of the Conqueror by His Secretary*, from *the Istoria De La Conquista De Mexico*, 1552 (Berkeley, Calif.: University of California Press, 1965) p 141

[v] Hernando Cortes, *Five Letters 1519-1526*, trans J. Bayard Morris (New York: W.W. Norton and Co., Inc., 1928) pp 21-22

[vi] Gomara, p 54

[vii] Ibid, p 142

[viii] Basil Davidson, *The Lost Cities of Africa*, first printed 1959 (New York: Little, Brown anc Company, 1987) pp 74-75

[ix] Ivan Van Sertima, *They Came Before Columbus: The African Presence in Ancient America* (New York: Random House, 1976) p 48

[x] Miguel Leon-Portilla, ed., *The Broken Spears*, trans Lysander Kemp (Boston: Beacon Press, 1962) p xv

[xi] William H. Prescott, *History of the Conquest of Mexico and History of the Conquest of Peru* (New York: Random House, Inc.) pp 15-16

[xii] Duran, p 16

[xiii] D.T. Niane, *Sundiata, An Epic of Old Mali,* trans G.D. Pickett (London: Longman Group Limited, 1965) p 85

[xiv] Bernal Diaz del Castillo, *The Discovery and Conquest of Mexico 1517-1521*, ed Genaro Garcia, trans A.P. Maudslay (New York: Farrar, Straus, and Cuhady, 1956) p 150
[xv] William Prescott, *History of the Conquest of Mexico & History of the Conquest of Peru,* reprinted in Modern Library (New York: Random House) pp 59-60

[xvi] Prescott, p 638 footnote 24

[xvii] Prescott, p 82

[xviii] Linda Schele and David Freidel, *A Forest of Kings* (New York: William Morrow, 1990) p 486 n. 20

[xix] Prescott, pp 52-53

[xx] Fray Diego Duran, *The Aztecs: The History of the Indies of New Spain*, trans Doris Heyden and Fernando Horcasitas (New York: Orion Press, Inc., 1964) pp 6-10

[xxi] J. Jorge Klor de Alva, H.B. Nicholson and Eloise Quinones Keber, *The Work of Bernardino de Sahagun: Pioneer Ethnographer of Sixteenth-Century Aztec Mexico*, ed Richard M. Leventhal and J. Jorge Klor de Alva (New York: Institute for Mesoamerican Studies, State University of New York, 1988) pp 184-186

[xxii] Ibid., pp 187-188

[xxiii] Heinrich Brugsch-Bey, *Egypt Under the Pharaohs* (London: John Murray, 1902, reprinted Random House UK Ltd, 1996) p 410

[xxiv] Kathleen Berrin and Esther Pasztory, eds., *Teotihuacan: Art from the City of the Gods* (New York: Thames and Hudson, 1993) p 157

[xxv] James Henry Breasted, ed. and trans., *Ancient Records of Egypt* (New York: Russell & Russell, Inc., 1906, reprinted 1962) vol iii, sect. 406

[xxvi] Breasted., vol iii, footnote f, page 192

[xxvii] Ibid., vol. iii, footnote a, page 195

[xxviii] Brugsch-Bey, p 356

[xxix] Ibid., p 355

[xxx] Breasted, vol. iv, sect. 565

[xxxi] Herodotus, *The Histories*, bk ii, sect. 124

[xxxii] Herodotus, *The Histories*, bk ii, sect. 149

[xxxiii] Brugsch-Bey, *Egypt Under the Pharaohs*, pg 77

[xxxiv] Kathleen Berrin and Esther Pasztory, Teotihuacan: Art from the City of the Gods, p 24

[xxxv] Ibid., pp 18, 77

[xxxvi] Brugsch-Bey, p14

[xxxvii] Godley, bk ii, sect. 125, p 427

[xxxviii] Ibid., pp 458-459

[xxxix] Herodotus, *Herodotus*, trans A.D. Godley (Cambridge, Mass: Harvard University Press, 1920, reprinted 1981) bk ii, sect 147-149, pp 455-459

[xl] Berrin and Pasztory, p 92

[xli] Berrin and Pasztory, p 96

[xlii] Adolf Erman, *Life in Ancient Egypt*, trans. H.M. Tirard (London: Macmillan and Company, 1894, reprinted Dover Publications, 1971) p 27

[xliii] Erman, pp 25-26

[xliv] Ibid., p 22

[xlv] Ibid., p 22

[xlvi] Brugsch-Bey, p 22, citing *Relation de Egypte*, translated by S. de Sacy

[xlvii] Godley, bk ii, sect 99, pp 385-387

[xlviii] Budge, p 11

[xlix] Burland, pp 55-58

[l] Burland, p 14
[li] Prescott, pp 458-459

[lii] Berrin and Pasztory, Teotihuacan, pg 22

[liii] Van Sertima, pp 47-48

[liv] Breasted, vol I, sect. 493

[lv] Map titled, "L'America: divis a Ne Suoi Principali State, Di Nuova Projezione, Venezia 1770. Preffo Antonio Zatta.
[lvi] Budge, pp 24-26

[lvii] Budge, p 26

[lviii] Brugsch-Bey, p 96

[lix] Brugsch-Bey, pp 96-97

[lx] Brugsch-Bey, p 98
[lxi] Josephus, "Antiquities of the Jews," bk vii, chap iii, sect 2, p 210

[lxii] Ibid., footnote, p 210

[lxiii] Ibid., chapter vii sect. 2

[lxiv] Brugsch-Bey, p 23

[lxv] Josephus "Antiquities of the Jews," bk vii, chap iii, footnote, page 210

[lxvi] Breasted, vol. iv, par. 117, p 69

[lxvii] Brugsch-Bey, p 4

[lxviii] Benjamin of Tudela, *The Itinerary of Benjamin of Tudela: Travels in the Middle Ages*, as translated from *Masa 'ot shel Rabi Binyamin* (New York: Joseph Simon, 1983, limited ed.) p 82

[lxix] Josephus, bk v, chapter iv

CPSIA information can be obtained at www.ICGtesting.com
Printed in the USA
BVOW041249160513

320905BV00001B/1/P